Who Wants to be a Dundonian?

Film-maker and best-selling author of *Dundonian for Beginners*, MICK McCLUSKEY began writing at the City Lit in London and shortly expanded his work to include stage, books and film and TV production. As well as spending thousands of hours as a freelance video camera operator on everything from human embryos to football cup finals, he has written and directed dramas, documentaries and training films, and two of his films have enjoyed cinema release.

Who Wants to be a
Dundonian?

Mick McCluskey

Black & White Publishing

First published 2002
by Black & White Publishing Ltd
99 Giles Street, Edinburgh EH6 6BZ

ISBN 1 902927 47 8

Copyright © Mick McCluskey 2002

The right of Mick McCluskey to be identified as the author of this
work has been asserted by him in accordance with the Copyright,
Designs and Patents Act 1988.

A CIP catalogue record for this book is available
from The British Library.

Cover design by McCusker Graphic Media

Printed and bound by Nørhaven Paperback A/S, Viborg Denmark

Contents

Introduction

I've often wondered what it is that makes someone into a Dundonian. Not that I've lost any sleep over it, I'm not that obsessive, but the question does beg an answer.

My own claim to be a Dundonian is the fact that I was born, schooled and apprenticed all within a half-mile radius of the hilly scheme of St Marys. The obvious give-away occurs as soon as I open my gub. 'Eh'll hay a peh' became a daily utterance of mine (or 'miynz') ever since I started dodging the school dinners and began nipping up to the baker's instead. Just loiter about in the doorway of any baker's in the city and you'll hear this spilling out of the mouths of almost everyone.

Maybe you were born, schooled and apprenticed in another city and moved to Dundee donkeys' years ago. Would you class yourself as a Dundonian? Would others class you as a Dundonian?

If you were a constipated mathematician, you might be able to work it all out using a pencil and, of course, paper. But that might take time. This book will endeavour to cut to the chase.

Who wants to be a Dundonian? is the quiz book that no Dundonian can afford to be without. It's the Lochee litmus test. Five hundred definitive questions designed to expose the True Dundonians from the Would-be, the Real-deal from the Kiddee-ons and the Schemeephiles from the Anglophiles.

Read on and find out if you are a true Dundonian.

Good luck!
Mick

Acknowledgements

I wish to thank Alan Shanyinde for his many hours of book-worming during the research and compilation of this book, and for his dedication to the project.

And, for many extras of juicy bits and bobs, I would like to thank Brian Whytock.

I would also like to thank Penny Clarke and everyone at Black & White Publishing for commissioning the book in the first place and for showing great enthusiasm throughout.

Dedicated to my son, Croy.
Born 2001,
a 21st-century Dundonian.

THE QUESTIONS

1

Nooadayz

Dundee nowadays is much like any other post-industrial city. Vast expanses of brownfield sites are being set upon by pieces of public art, intent on bringing a bit of culture to an otherwise derelict skelp of land. Newcastle, Liverpool, Glasgow and Dundee, not to mention the others, have transformed themselves from depressed monocultures to communities in favour of international cultural exhibits, expensive cafés, and a happy change from the drudgery of the past.

Dundee's explosion in adult education has helped to fuel the cultural change in the city and, combined with Further Education placements being in the region of 21,000, it's hardly a surprise. Nooadayz there are more Dundonians in full-time adult education today than in any other period in the city's history.

Having said all that, most Dundonians live a fair distance from the 'spoilt' city centre areas of the Waterfront and the West End, and some never venture into these areas from one year to the next. After all, the likes of Whitfield, Douglas and Lochee have very little in common with the 'spiyult kwartir'. Not surprisingly, you won't see many West End residents or fresher students heading out to those areas in search of an entertaining evening out.

Some things, however, don't change. Saturday nights, for example, are still the prime time to get rat-arsed drunk and make a complete arse of yourself if you're of a certain age, and the city still has a plethora of pubs and clubs to choose from if you are inclined to this sort of activity.

Until recently, Dundee had one of the best pub music scenes in the country, where you could get high on Dundee soul almost every night of the week. Now that the emphasis has changed from pubs to arts, you are more likely to hear jazz or folk music played live. The places for live music might have become thin on the ground but the local musicians themselves are still in melodic abundance, waiting in the wings for the regeneration of the local music venues.

1.1 Which housing scheme does the 'Black Watch Soldier' watch over?

a	Kirkton	c	Fintry
b	Charleston	d	Menzieshill

1.2 What is Stobsmuir Park better known as?

a	Campay	c	Cairdee
b	Swanny Ponds	d	Magdalen Green

1.3 What stands atop the highest point of the 'Law'?

a	A radio mast	c	A war memorial
b	An Iron-Age fort	d	A drunk

1.4 Where is the Hilltown Clock?

a	Dudhope Terrace	c	Hill Street
b	Constitution Road	d	Strathmartine Road

1.5 Where is 'The Dundee Pie Shop'?

a	Lochee	c	Hilltown
b	Nethergate	d	Old Glamis Road

1.6 How many tower blocks comprise the Alexander Street multies?

a	Four	c	Six
b	Three	d	Eight

1.7 Which is a genuine Derby Street multi?

a	Bucklemaker	c	Ferret Strangler
b	Sheep Sh***er	d	Dowp Skelper

1.8 Which city park has a cannon in its grounds?

a	Camperdown	c	Baxter
b	Dudhope	d	Clatto

1.9 Which former mill still has a WW2 fortification on its roof?

a	Windmill	c	Meadowmill
b	Watermill	d	Hillmill

1.10 Which school is now located in Dudhope Castle?

a	Dundee Business School	c	Dundee Correction School
b	Dundee Pochlers Academy	d	University of Silly Walks

1.11 Which port is farthest from the river?

a	Northport	c	Southport
b	Glessaport	d	Westport

1.12 Name the gate from the old walled city which still remains standing?

a	Colgate	c	Parkgate
b	Cowgate	d	Goatgate

1.13 What is the name of the longest lane in Broughty Ferry?

a	Long Lane	c	Sma Lane
b	Lovers Lane	d	Lois Lane

1.14 Which is Britain's only full-time public observatory?

a	Universal Watchery	c	Mills Observatory
b	Star Lookery	d	Moon Gazery

1.15 And which hill does it sit atop?

a	Craigowl	c	Barnowl
b	Balgay	d	Whazgay

1.16 When did it open for business?

a	1935	c	1925
b	1915	d	1945

1.17 Which faculty of Dundee University is housed in the Wellcome Trust building?

a	Arts and Social Science	c	Biomedical
b	Information Technology	d	Faculty of forgotten Sciences

1.18 What kind of shop is in the Morgan Tower?

a	A bookie's	c	A pub
b	A bookshop	d	A pharmacy

1.19 The NCR is situated in which estate?

a	Gourdie	c	Greedy
b	Grumpy	d	Grippy

1.20 On what brae does the Black Watch Memorial stand?

a	Chocolate Brae	c	Powrie Brae
b	Steep Brae	d	Bentley's Brae

1.21 Which tyre factory came to Baldovie in 1972?

a	Dunlop	c	Michelin
b	Mould-a-lot	d	Paid-a-lot

1.22 In which 'Park' can you find whale's teeth?

a	Caird Park	c	Lochee Park
b	Dens Park	d	Polepark

1.23 What's the name of the leisure centre at the waterfront?

a	Olympia	c	Olympica
b	Orangea	d	The Baths

1.24 And what is berthed close to it?

a	A replica of the Tay Whale	c	The Lord Provost's Yacht
b	RSS *Discovery*	d	A three-berth caravan

1.25 What do Dundonian seagulls rarely eat?

a	Pizza	c	Pakuras
b	Chips, cheese and mayonnaise	d	Freshly caught fish

1.26 What do Dundonian teenagers rarely eat?

| a | Pizza | c | Pakuras |
| b | Chips, cheese and mayonnaise | d | Freshly caught fish |

1.27 How many Starbucks are there in Dundee?

| a | 2 | c | 3 |
| b | 1 | d | Too many |

1.28 Name the Michael Marra song considered by many to be Scotland's new national anthem?

| a | 'Baldness' | c | 'Hermless' |
| b | 'Toughness' | d | 'Breekless' |

1.29 What is The Circus?

| a | A roundabout | c | A big-top over the City Square |
| b | A nightclub | d | A dayclub for pensioners |

1.30 Which university did the entertainer St Andrew claim to have studied at?

| a | Sky High (or 'Skeh Heh') | c | Aberwheechter |
| b | Boxford | d | Cambridge |

1.31 Who are the Hazey Janes?

a	A dance troop	c	A group of glamour models
b	A support group for contact lens wearers	d	A group of musicians

1.32 Which actor's odyssey was Salem to Moscow?

a	Robert Robertson	c	Brian Cox
b	Sean Connery	d	Stanley Baxter

1.33 Who founded the Dundee Guitar Festival?

a	Alan Bretenbach	c	Allan Neave
b	Chris Marra	d	Gregor Philp

1.34 Which West Kirkton laddie grew up to conduct the Dundee People's Orchestra?

a	Kevin Murray	c	Gordon MacPherson
b	Herb Alpert	d	Chopin

1.35 What stands on the ground where the now demolished 1960s Overgate shopping centre once stood?

a	A new shop-lined street with each proprietor wearing a clean apron	c	A bingo hall
b	Another Overgate shopping centre	d	A city centre park

1.36 Who is considered to be the godfather of Dundee soul?

a	Alan Gorrie	c	Dougie Martin
b	Michael Marra	d	Jack Bruce

1.37 And which long-running band does he sing with?

a	Average White Band	c	Mafia
b	The Woollen Mill	d	Cream

1.38 What was Dundee poet Don Paterson's first collection of poems called?

a	*Nil Nil*	c	*One All*
b	*Two's Up*	d	*Nuhinz Up*

1.39 Name the Lochee bingo club which once was a cinema.

a	The Rizotto	c	The Ronaldo
b	The Ricardo	d	The Rialto

1.40 Jim McLean resigned his chairmanship of Dundee United after being caught on TV doing what?

a	Playing keepy-up wi' the books	c	Hitting a BBC reporter
b	Swearing at the Queen	d	Leaving a brothel

1.41 How much is an adult lower-tier ticket to Tannadice?

a	£16	c	£5.50
b	£25	d	£20

1.42 How much is an adult centre-stand ticket to Dens Park?

a	£13	c	£9.50
b	£17	d	£21

1.43 Where would Broughty Ferry ice-cream parlour connoisseurs go?

a	Vandal's	c	Viking's
b	Verdigri's	d	Visocchi's

1.44 Where would you find the Phoenix?

a	In the ashes	c	Having a blether with Sinbad
b	In a nest	d	In the Nethergate

1.45 In what 'House' would you find karaoke?

a	Town House	c	Sea Captain's House
b	My House	d	S***e House

1.46 Where would you find the Little Theatre?

a	Bellfield Street	c	Victoria Road
b	Tay Square	d	Where you would find little actors

1.47 Who wrote the stage play *On the Line*?

a	Alan Spence	c	Gordon Burnside
b	Chris Rattray	d	Billy Kay

1.48 And who wrote the music?

a	Kevin Murray	c	Michael Marra
b	Ricky Ross	d	Derek Thomson

1.49 *On the Line* was about life in which Dundee factory?

a	NCR	c	The Coffin Mill
b	Keillers	d	Timex

1.50 What is 'The Word on the Pavey'?

a	An album	c	A slaiver
b	A big daft gowk	d	Keech

2

The Language

The language of the average Dundonian, esoteric in its very nature, obscure in its delivery, with a faint whiff of strangulation is, to me, sweet music, mother's bosom and a deep comfort in the knowledge that I can talk about the world as only a Dundonian can understand it.

The origin of the local language remains unclear. Some do say that it has, in fact, derived from an actual Scottish source. Others may say that the language was handed down from spacemen. But they mostly turn out to live in Whitfield and have Elvis as a next-door neighbour, so I wouldn't exactly take their word for it if I were you.

There's a certain school of thought that believes that the treacherous conditions in the linen, flax and jute mills of bygone years were to blame for the butchering of certain words – a result of trying to hold a conversation throughout the deafening clatter of nearby machinery, so it's said. Personally, I hold sway with the Wallace theory. Not Wallace as in *Braveheart* fame but of the shortcrust pastry variety.

'What's that you're baking?' a posh voice asked.

Wallace, being a baker and Dundonian answered, 'Pehz!' He was mispronouncing on account of recently becoming completely toothless, as a result of an encounter with an over-baked Forfar bridie earlier in the day.

'Oh,' said the posh voice. 'In that case, I'll have twa!'

2.1 What would your feet be if they were 'bowfin'?

a	Pedicured	c	Flat
b	Smelly	d	Shoeless

2.2 What would you be if you were 'harnekit'?

a	A decent chap	c	Off the deep end
b	A chancer	d	A council worker

2.3 What is a 'dockay'?

a	A rock	c	A female
b	A window cleaner	d	A dock worker

2.4 What is a 'scaffay'?

a	A fish supper	c	A scalding cup of tea
b	A bartender	d	A refuse collector

2.5 If you were to receive a 'skelp', what would you get?

a	A Pools win	c	A smack
b	A New Year kiss	d	The sack

2.6 If you were 'ruftin', what would you be doing?

a	Running	c	Being cheeky
b	Belching	d	Breaking wind

2.7 What would Dundonians call a makeshift bed?

a	A shakaydoon	c	A kippy-up
b	A skeky	d	A makeshift bed

2.8 If you were 'fehntin', what would you be doing?

a	Resting	c	Drooling
b	Singing	d	Fainting

2.9 What is the local word for a puddle?

a	A pool	c	A lochlet
b	A re-mix	d	A dub

2.10 If someone was 'crabbit', what would they be?

a	Bad tempered	c	Bad breathed
b	A bad whistler	d	Bad and ugly

2.11 What kind of bird is a 'doo'?

| a | A seagull | c | A sparrow |
| b | A buzzard | d | A pigeon |

2.12 What is a roadside drain commonly known as?

| a | A creepy | c | A cundee |
| b | A crappy | d | A keechy |

2.13 What would you be doing if you were 'cowpin' something?

| a | Eating it | c | Scratching it |
| b | Tipping it | d | Feeling it |

2.14 Where is your 'dowp'?

| a | Your chin | c | Your nose |
| b | Your bum | d | Your bedroom |

2.15 What is another name for very dirty?

| a | Cheepit | c | Meowit |
| b | Woofit | d | Barkit |

2.16 What do you call someone that talks a lot of nonsense?

a	A slaiver	c	A hayvir
b	A craver	d	A bloomin' pest

2.17 If you took the 'boak', what would you be feeling?

a	Smart	c	Thick
b	Sick	d	Cocky

2.18 If something was 'pyuchy', what would it be?

a	Deathly slow	c	Horrible and sickly
b	Nice and soft	d	Too loud

2.19 Where indoors would you hang your washing?

a	A pushee	c	A poofee
b	A pansy	d	A poolee

2.20 Where would you go to get a 'stookee'?

a	A pub	c	A fun fair
b	A retirement home	d	A hospital

2.21 If you were told you were 'dytit', what would you be?

| a | Shy | c | Stupid |
| b | Sneaky | d | Soaking |

2.22 What does 'hakit' mean?

| a | Most beautiful | c | Pot-ugly |
| b | Full-bellied | d | Full o' wind |

2.23 What is a 'chantay'?

| a | Part of a set of bagpipes | c | A bottle of perfume |
| b | A toilet | d | A river channel |

2.24 What is an experienced fruit picker called?

| a | A necker | c | A nosy |
| b | A nicker | d | A nabbler |

2.25 What is another name for an alley?

| a | A pokay | c | A pehnday |
| b | A pichay | d | A poofee |

2.26 If something was 'gugget', what would it be?

a	Rotten	c	Rickety
b	Roasting	d	Rabid

2.27 If you had the 'feechee touch', what would you be?

a	Rich	c	Poor
b	Able to turn water into Buckfast	d	Contagious

2.28 What is a person of lowly status called?

a	A neep	c	A ned
b	A nymph	d	A nyaff

2.29 What would you describe as 'mingin'?

a	A breeze of fresh air	c	My onion (as in peh)
b	A sweet-smelling aroma	d	The fragrance of a sewage worker

2.30 If you were 'dirlin', what would you be doing?

a	Waving	c	Vibrating
b	Running	d	Shouting

2.31 What is a 'chappy-up'?

a	A late evening meal	c	A tin of dog food on a high shelf
b	An early morning call	d	A midnight spew

2.32 What would you call a witlessly frightened person?

a	A pee-the-bed	c	A fairdeegowk
b	A skitter-the-kilt	d	A piykir

2.33 What is a 'fleg'?

a	A fish	c	A fart
b	A finger	d	A fright

2.34 If you were 'glaikit', what would you be wearing?

a	A new coat	c	A black eye
b	A vacant facial expression	d	A medal of honour

2.35 What is a 'pletty'?

a	A tenement walkway	c	A narrow pavement
b	A church pew	d	A muddy path

2.36 If you were to be accused of being a 'slahbir', what would you be doing?

a	Throttling something	c	Squeezing something
b	Crushing something	d	Spilling something

2.37 What does 'Dah ken' mean?

a	Don't be so daft, Ken!	c	My dad's name is Ken.
b	I know the answer, it's Ken!	d	I haven't a clue.

2.38 What is a 'haf-pan'?

a	A leg of mutton	c	A loaf of bread
b	A poor soul	d	A halfwit

2.39 What would you be doing if you were being 'pan loafay'?

a	Talking shop	c	Talking s**te
b	Talking posh	d	Talking back

2.40 What would you be doing if you were heard to say, 'eech meech'?

a	Choking	c	Cheating
b	Chappin' (domino terminology)	d	Counting

2.41 And what comes next?

a	Hawks	c	Hens
b	Hoos	d	Hakit

2.42 If you were called a 'bizum', what would you be?

a	A thief	c	A soldier
b	A pest	d	A parrot

2.43 What would you be if you were 'pink lint'?

a	Sunburnt	c	Clean shaven
b	Scuffed	d	Skint

2.44 What is another name for 'locked'?

a	Spehckt	c	Snehct
b	Slept	d	Snapped

2.45 What is a 'spyugee'?

a	A sidekick	c	A shelter
b	A sponsor	d	A sparrow

2.46 If you were going to 'Cahmpay', where would you be going?

a	A camp site	c	Caird Park
b	Constitution Road	d	Camperdown Park

2.47 What is a 'jooblee'?

a	A sweet	c	A sour
b	A smack	d	A jobby

2.48 What is a 'kribee'?

a	A knot	c	A kerb
b	A kick	d	A kiss

2.49 If you were to give a child a 'shoagee-boagee', what would you be giving it?

a	A telling off	c	A reward
b	A rock	d	A roll

2.50 Complete the following – 'Eh'm ma ma'z ...'?

a	Big ugly bugger	c	Big schoopit erse
b	Big glaikit hack	d	Big bubbulee bairn

3

The Aldin Days

Dundee has had its fair share of good times and bad. In the past it's been set upon, torched, battered stupid, robbed, rebuilt, become wealthy, plundered, conferred upon, occupied and starved – and all that in its first week.

Since then it's been prosperous, set upon, torched, battered stupid, robbed, rebuilt, plundered, given its own saint, set upon again, occupied, half-starved, flea-bitten and ricket-ridden – until nooadayz, that is.

By all accounts, Dundee in the aldin days was a hotbed of sedition, patriotism, merchandising, political astuteness, cunning inventors and money. Oh yes, I almost forgot, the majority of its inhabitants were ordinary Dundonians who never (in my father's words) had 'twa hupnayz ti rub thi githir' but would never see somebody stuck without a bed for the night.

Since then, it has risen to be a proud city of sedition, patriotism, merchandising, political astuteness, cunning inventors and money. Although you might have to rub a few ten-pound notes together to be able to get a bed for the night.

The city has had a rich history of declaring folk kings, witches, blasphemers, jute barons, worthies and hapless poets. And that's just the tip of this esoteric iceberg of Dundonian declarations. Most outsiders fail to get to grip with the lingo and that's why most declarations seem to go unheard. Folk here have been declaring a variety of stuff on a nightly basis in the city ever since the invention of alcohol.

3.1 In 1949, a record crowd of 43,000 attended a football match between Dundee and Rangers. What was the final score?

a	Dundee 3 Rangers 1	c	Rangers 3 Dundee 1
b	The match was postponed	d	The match was abandoned

3.2 When was the war memorial erected on the Dundee Law?

a	1918	c	1942
b	1921	d	1882

3.3 Which Mary granted the Howff to Dundee?

a	Mary Magdalen	c	Mary Queen of Scots
b	Mary, Mary, quite contrary	d	Hairy Mary

3.4 Which association used the Howff as a meeting place until 1776?

a	Incorporated Fools	c	Incorporated Tools
b	Incontinent Bulls	d	Uncompromising Mules

3.5 What would 'fleshers' be more commonly known as today?

a	Sailors	c	Butchers
b	Pikers	d	Chancers

3.6 What does 'howff' mean?

| a | Remembering place | c | Moaning place |
| b | Meeting place | d | Chips and plaice |

3.7 Which of the following is *not* one of the 'Three United Trades'?

| a | Masons | c | Slaters |
| b | Pawnbrokers | d | Wrights |

3.8 What was the name of the Broughty Ferry cinema?

| a | The Regal | c | The Lambert and Butler |
| b | The Embassy | d | The Players |

3.9 Who, according to local folklore, was Grizzel Jaffray?

| a | A thief | c | A witch |
| b | A loaby dosser | d | A priest |

3.10 Where was the 'Bohbeez Helmet' located?

| a | On his head | c | At the top of the Wellgate steps |
| b | At the bottom of his trouser leg | d | In the middle of Meadowside |

3.11 Which city park has the 1 o'clock gun in its grounds?

a	Caird Park	c	Dudhope Park
b	Car Park	d	Clatto Park

3.12 Who granted Sir Alexander Scrymgeour the hereditary office of Constable of Dundee in 1298?

a	Sir William Wallace	c	Sir William Pieman
b	Sir Charlie Drake	d	Sir Bobby Sixfooter

3.13 Who said they would 'See the grass growing in the streets of Dundee' before they would return to the city?

a	Parky Tam	c	Queen Elizabeth II
b	Winston Churchill	d	King James I

3.14 What year did trams stop running in the city?

a	1955	c	1946
b	1965	d	1956

3.15 Who or what was 'The Proggie'?

a	A debt collector	c	A Masonic hall
b	A pub	d	A doctor

3.16 Which 'Mountains' housed a notorious slum?

a	White Mountains	c	Blue Mountains
b	Black and Blue Mountains	d	Red-raw Mountains

3.17 Which is *not* one of the 'Nine Trades'?

a	Weavers	c	Joiners
b	Bonnetmakers	d	Hammermen

3.18 Where did 'Heaven and Hell' share the same land?

a	Cowgate	c	Byregate
b	Sheepgate	d	Parkgate

3.19 What was 'Heaven and Hell'?

a	A chip shop	c	A church and a pub
b	An orphanage and a brothel	d	A bank

3.20 In which century was St Mary's Tower built?

a	12th	c	15th
b	19th	d	4th

3.21 Which 'William' embarked on his outlaw career by killing the son of the English governor?

a	William Tell	c	Oor Wullie
b	Willie Nokum (back again)	d	William Wallace

3.22 Who was pronounced 'King' at Dundee Castle?

a	Robert the Bruce	c	Charlie the Chicken
b	William Wallace	d	King Rollo

3.23 Which English general looted the city with his army in 1651?

a	General Monk	c	General Minister
b	General Motors	d	General Anesthetic

3.24 Name the Iron-Age Pictish fort which stood on the Law hill.

a	Dun Deagh	c	Dung Deagh
b	Tweedle Dee	d	Kiki Dee

3.25 What or who ran through the Law between 1820 and 1860?

a	Olympic runners	c	A railway line
b	A water main	d	A runaway outlaw

3.26 Name the brutal slayer who was reputed to have been killed by a silver bullet at the battle of Killicrankie?

a	John Graham of Claverhouse	c	Rab McCulloch of the Hilltown
b	Chic of Whitfield	d	Tom Walker of Broughty Ferry

3.27 What was his 'nice' nickname?

a	Barkit Dundee	c	Bosom Dundee
b	Bonny Dundee	d	Sunny Dundee

3.28 What was his popular and not-so-nice nickname?

a	Bloomin Slaivers	c	Bluidy Claivers
b	At The Capers	d	Big Haivers

3.29 Which 16th-century lord traitorously surrendered Broughty Ferry Castle to the English?

a	Lord of the Rings	c	Lord Green
b	Lord Gray	d	Lord Dundee

3.30 Name the Nethergate cinema which was converted to Mecca?

a	The Greens Playhouse	c	The Brown S**t House
b	The Red Itch House	d	The Black Scab House

3.31 Where was the Royal Arch situated?

| a | In the City Square | c | At the Cowgate |
| b | At the top of the Royal Legs | d | Beside King William Dock |

3.32 Which 19th-century member of Dundee's Reformed Parliament had been previously charged and outlawed for sedition?

| a | Rab Kinloch | c | Tam Kinloch |
| b | George Kinloch | d | John Kinloch |

3.33 What was the name of Dundee's last working carthorse?

| a | Pepe | c | Paddy |
| b | Poppy | d | Pee-wee |

3.34 What was St Mary's parish church originally known as?

| a | St Mary's in the Huff | c | St Mary's in the Water |
| b | St Mary's in the Club | d | St Mary's in the Field |

3.35 What hung from St Mary's Tower during Monk's occupation of the city?

| a | A thief's hand | c | A head |
| b | A pair of breeks | d | A lone glove |

3.36 And who did it belong to?

a	A witch	c	The town governor
b	A banker	d	The town constable

3.37 What was the old Town House Arcade known as?

a	The Posers	c	The Pests
b	The Pillars	d	The Pickpockets

3.38 Which 'burgh' was sold to Dundee in 1643?

a	Edinburgh	c	Jedburgh
b	Fraserburgh	d	Hilltown

3.39 At the beginning of the 20th century, Dundee had 582 what?

a	Pubs	c	Toilets
b	Backlands	d	Boglands

3.40 By 1901, where did almost three out of four Dundee families live?

a	Tents	c	1–2 roomed houses
b	3–4 roomed houses	d	Bungalows

3.41 By the end of the 19th century, Dundee had the country's highest what?

a	Infant mortality rate	c	IQ level
b	Opinion of itself	d	Number of prostitutes

3.42 In 1669, what completely destroyed the old Dundee Harbour?

a	Fire	c	A tempest
b	A wee laddie	d	A crooked councillor's demolition firm

3.43 Which Scots king picked a fight with the local Picts in 730 and raised his standard upon the King's Cross?

a	Alexander	c	Elvis
b	Alpin	d	Wheetabix

3.44 And what happened next?

a	The Scots beheaded the Picts	c	The Picts beheaded the king on the King's Cross
b	The Scots ran away singing 'Eh'm ma ma's big bubblee bairn'	d	They all agreed to peace and had a game of dominos

3.45 What is King's Cross?

a	A railway station	c	A small piece of volcanic glass
b	A place of contagion	d	A large stone with a circular hole

3.46 Which musician once lived in the Hilltown?

a	Charlotte Church	c	Lulu
b	Jimmy Shand	d	Grand Master Flash

3.47 Which Dundonian attempted to compile a dictionary in fifty languages?

a	James Bowman Lindsay	c	William McGonagall
b	Tom Moore	d	William Wallace

3.48 What did The Theatre Royal used to be called?

a	His Majesty's	c	The Palace Theatre
b	The Scratcher	d	The Playhouse

3.49 In which road was the Tivoli Theatre situated?

a	Mains Road	c	Alexander Street
b	Paradise Road	d	Bonnybank Road

3.50 Which building was called 'The Proggie'?

a	The Progress Hall	c	The Prostitute Palace
b	The Progressive Dosshouse	d	The Peelee-Wally Emporium

4

The River

The River Tay has always been a magnet that pulls Dundonians into its tidal heartbeat. It doesn't matter where you may live in the city, the lure of the shining water will inevitably cast its spell on you. And you, like the flounders in its depths, will be hooked. The only down side of the river that I have came across is that it somehow always manages to sneak some sand into your pieces when your back is turned, even when you're looking at it through binoculars from the top of the Law hill.

Dundonian kids are often compelled to throw stones at the river and sometimes even try their luck at the seals. Hearing the plop or the yelp must somehow manage to cement their bond with the river in a way only a child can understand. However, whether 'plopping' with dockayz or throwing skimmers, the river will eventually repay you one day – probably in the guise of a few grains of sand in your unsuspecting cheese piece. The river may be many things but daft it certainly is not.

If it weren't for the river, there would probably be no Dundee and no stone-throwing Dundonian kids living on its banks. If it weren't for the river we would undoubtedly have nowhere to flush our toilets. If it weren't for the river none of us would be here. We'd probably be living in (God forbid) Forfar or (worse) Aberdeen. If it weren't for the river, Dundonians would no doubt be up some other river without a paddle. Although I can't imagine them making up songs about the 'Silvery Dee', can you?

4.1 What warship was docked in the city from 1869–1929?

a	*Mars*	c	*Jupiter*
b	*Neptune*	d	*Pluto*

4.2 Who were kept there?

a	Single mothers	c	Destitute boys
b	Greetin' faces	d	Fallen virgins

4.3 Where does the Tay Whale now reside?

a	In the Tay	c	In the McManus Galleries
b	At Dundee University	d	In a series of bottles

4.4 What sex was the Whale?

a	Male	c	Female
b	Asexual	d	Sex o' tatties

4.5 What was played on the river's sandbanks at low tide?

a	Kissy-catchy	c	Feelee-fo
b	Tennis	d	Football

4.6 Who plays there now?

| a | The Dundee Whalers | c | Dundee FC |
| b | Seals | d | Bairns |

4.7 What was 'The Fifie'?

| a | A chip shop | c | A ferryboat |
| b | A pub | d | A church |

4.8 The Tay Road Bridge opened in which year?

| a | 1966 | c | 1967 |
| b | 1969 | d | 1976 |

4.9 When did the original Tay Rail Bridge open?

| a | 1899 | c | 1878 |
| b | 1978 | d | 1909 |

4.10 When did it blow down?

| a | 1879 | c | 1900 |
| b | 1966 | d | 1887 |

4.11 The RSS *Discovery* was built for which expedition?

a	Arctic	c	Moon landing
b	Antarctic	d	Discovery channel

4.12 When was it launched?

a	1967	c	1976
b	1899	d	1901

4.13 And who was the captain?

a	Captain Kirk	c	Captain Pugwash
b	Captain Scarlet	d	Captain Scott

4.14 Name the oldest British-built ship still afloat.

a	*Unicorn*	c	*Peppercorn*
b	*Fulacorn*	d	*Saircorn*

4.15 What kind of ship is it?

a	A cruise ship	c	A yacht
b	A space ship	d	A war ship

4.16 Which riverside walkway was opened in 1875?

a	Tay Lane	c	River Walk
b	Esplanade	d	Orangeade

4.17 Which of the following has *never* been a Dundee dock?

a	King William IV Dock	c	Dock Stewart's
b	Victoria Dock	d	Earl Grey Dock

4.18 Name the shipping company which started running a twice-weekly service to London and Glasgow in 1826?

a	DP& L	c	QRS&T
b	P&O	d	S&M

4.19 Which '—*shire*' ran aground while steaming from Hull to Dundee?

a	*Wilt*	c	*Aberdeen*
b	*Perth*	d	*Forfar*

4.20 Who was the heroine that, along with her father, rowed out in stormy weather to save nine lives from the stricken vessel?

a	Grace Darling	c	Grace Honey
b	Grace Sugar-Plum	d	Grace Sweetheart

4.21 What was the name of the last ship-building yard in Dundee?

a	The Robb Caledon	c	The Jock Tamson
b	The Elton John	d	The Bob Scalding

4.22 Name the last whaling ship to be built in the city?

a	The Nutty Slack	c	The Terra Nova
b	The Peek-a-Boo	d	The Whale Eater

4.23 What is the third-oldest ship in the world that still remains afloat?

a	The Arc	c	The Dodo
b	The Phoenix	d	The Unicorn

4.24 What pier did the *Fifie* leave from?

a	Craig Pier	c	Crag Pier
b	Cross Pier	d	Crumb Pier

4.25 In 1903, the *Terra Nova* and which other Dundee whaling ship were sent to rescue Captain Scott's *Discovery* from the Antarctic ice?

a	Evening	c	Midnight
b	Morning	d	Afternoon

4.26 Name the ship that eventually took Captain Scott on his fateful journey to the Antarctic in 1910?

a	*Discovery*	c	*The Terra Nova*
b	*The Santa Maria*	d	*The Jonah*

4.27 Which of the following is the earliest known name for the River Tay?

a	Tow	c	Tee
b	Ta	d	Silvery

4.28 And what does it mean?

a	To thank	c	To melt or flow
b	A place to fish	d	The deep

4.29 What happened when merchants tried to take their grain-laden ships out of Dundee harbour to sell it at a higher profit elsewhere, while the town was starving in 1773?

a	The crews refused to set sail	c	They were stopped by the authorities
b	They were looted by the locals	d	They had a change of heart and gave their grain to the starving

4.30 From which loch does the river originate?

a	Loch Earn	c	Loch Brandy
b	Loch Lomond	d	Loch Tay

4.31 How many seals did the *Terra Nova* kill on its maiden voyage?

a	25,734	c	432
b	12 (pups not included)	d	163,276

4.32 For approximately how many centuries did Dundee kill whales on an industrial scale?

a	Two	c	One
b	Five	d	Four

4.33 How many freshwater lochs does the Tay drain?

a	160	c	70
b	50	d	14

4.34 In which month did whalers traditionally leave Dundee?

a	January	c	June
b	September	d	April

4.35 How far does the Tay flow from its farthest source to the North Sea?

a	117 miles	c	385 miles
b	98 miles	d	47 miles

4.36 Where was Dundee's first floating dock opened in 1824?

a	King Alexander Wharf	c	King Charles' Dock
b	King Tutt's Dock	d	King William's Wharf

4.37 Which of the following was *not* a major export from Dundee in the 17th century?

a	Hides	c	Wine
b	Wool	d	Sheepskin

4.38 The Dundee–Baltic shipping lanes were used by hundreds of ships during the 17th and 18th centuries. What percentage of them were Scottish ships?

a	15%	c	60%
b	3%	d	75%

4.39 When did the current Tay Rail Bridge open?

a	1883	c	1983
b	1902	d	1887

4.40 William McGonagall wrote an ode to the new bridge. What was it called?

a	'Address to the new Tay Bridge'	c	'Back Across the Silvery Tay'
b	'An Ode to the Tay Bridge'	d	'That'll Dae the Tay'

4.41 Which of the following was *never* a Dundee shipbuilding yard?

| a | Gourlay's | c | Thompson's |
| b | Brown & Simpson | d | Arm & Legg |

4.42 How much did the *Discovery* cost to construct?

| a | £643,000 | c | £51,000 |
| b | £3,200 | d | £89,000 |

4.43 Who led the Dutch fleet at the battle of Camperdown?

| a | Admiral Duncan | c | Admiral van Summer |
| b | Admiral de Winter | d | Admiral d'Autumn |

4.44 When was the first iron ship built in Dundee?

| a | 1854 | c | 1899 |
| b | 1798 | d | 1926 |

4.45 How much did John Woods pay for the Tay Whale?

| a | £50 | c | £226 |
| b | £149 | d | £75 |

4.46 And what did he do with his whale?

a	He charged Dundonians to view it	c	He gave it away to hungry street kids
b	He ate it himself	d	He sold it as sausages

4.47 When did HM frigate *Unicorn* begin its stay in Dundee harbour?

a	1973	c	1873
b	1923	d	1893

4.48 Which riverside centre does the RGIT Montrose run?

a	The Science Centre	c	The Olympia
b	Marine Training Centre	d	Oil-drilling Training Centre

4.49 Which local hero was the sole survivor of one of 'The Chieftain's' boats when it ran into fog near Greenland in 1884?

a	Jock Tamson	c	Joey Mahoey
b	Jasper Carrot	d	James McIntosh

4.50 And how many extra children did he go on to have despite losing both his legs?

a	1	c	7
b	9	d	4

5

Doon Toon

Although Dundee has been a city for a fair few years now, it's still managed to retain the template of a small town. Some folk head for the 'city centre' to soak up the metropolitan atmosphere but most folk simply go 'doon the toon' for a dander. The fact that you can walk from one end of the city centre to the other in around ten minutes adds extra weight to the struggle between city and town, and, if you happen to be caught up in conversation as you walk, you can easily find yourself in and out of the metropolis without even noticing that you have actually been there.

In a little over thirty years, the centre of Dundee has gone from a bustling archaic treasure of narrow medieval streets and wynds, where love and rickets strolled hand in hand and the feral wildlife rarely starved, to a place where pavements and pedestrian precincts rule supreme and even the dooz have difficulty finding a suitable home. People and dooz were hastily evicted to make way for the modern age of shopping centres to come to the city and, with corrosive swiftness, the bulldozers had done their job, the corrupt officials had done their time and the Dundonians were just plain 'done'.

One thing is certain – there's more sunlight reaching the city centre streets nowadays than at any other time in the past. And that's bound to be a good thing for everybody. Perhaps with the exception of newborn babes and bald-headed men.

And what's to become of our dearly beloved 'doon toon'? Will the architecture change to reflect the growth in cultural diversity and give us pagodas and the like, or will international arrivals become assimilated like the Irish immigration of previous generations, slotting neatly into tenement life of the 21st century?

One thing is certain – they'll be able to enjoy the sunshine while walking the city streets. Especially if they wear a hat.

5.1 How high is the Old Steeple?

a	156 yards	c	156 feet
b	156 metres	d	156 inches

5.2 When did the 'new' Overgate Centre open for business?

a	1999	c	2000
b	2001	d	1998

5.3 Where is there a memorial to the fallen Dundonian volunteers of the International Brigade?

a	City Square	c	Fiveways Circle
b	Jamaica Square	d	Albert Square

5.4 Which city centre mill is now a working museum?

a	Cox's Mill	c	Tay Works
b	Verdant Works	d	Tam Dizna Work

5.5 Where is Sea Captain's House?

a	St Andrews	c	St Andrews Street
b	St Andrews Lane	d	St Andrew and the Woollen Mill's gang hutty

5.6 What piece of musical charm is hazardously cemented into the pavement in St Andrews street?

a	A trumpet	c	A kazoo
b	A piano	d	A bell

5.7 How many statues stand in Albert Square?

a	4	c	5
b	6	d	3

5.8 Who accompanies Desperate Dan and his dog on the corner of Reform Street?

a	Dennis the Menace	c	Minnie the Minx
b	The Bash Street Kids	d	His auntie

5.9 How many fountains are in City Square?

a	6	c	5
b	3	d	2

5.10 Which of the following is *not* written on the plaques on the City Square water fountains?

a	Earth	c	Wind
b	Fire	d	Water

5.11 To whom were the McManus Galleries dedicated?

| a | Mick McManus | c | Dirk Gently |
| b | Robert the Bruce | d | Prince Albert |

5.12 Which office did the 'Circus' take over?

| a | The Post Office | c | The Office of Fair Trading |
| b | The Sheriff's Office(rs) | d | The Office for the Liberation of Captive Animals |

5.13 Who has his likeness outside St Paul's Episcopal Cathedral?

| a | Corporal Punishment | c | Admiral Duncan |
| b | Captain Scarlet | d | Private Parts |

5.14 Which Dundee street was blown out of rock in the 1780s?

| a | Dock Street | c | Castle Street |
| b | The High Street | d | Lochee Road |

5.15 How many bronze architecture models stand outside Boots and the Overgate?

| a | 3 | c | 16 |
| b | 9 | d | 1 |

5.16 Outside which pub would you see a model of the Old Town House?

a	Tickety Boo's	c	Counting House
b	Caw's Bar	d	The Pillars

5.17 What time does the 'Hickory Dickory' Gate show?

a	Tea time	c	Ten to eight
b	Quarter to six	d	Twenty past one

5.18 What was Seagate formerly known as?

a	St Mary's Gate	c	Robert the Bruce Gate
b	Hell's Gate	d	Dock Street

5.19 What were the McManus Galleries originally built as?

a	The City Institute for sexual deviants	c	A school
b	The Albert Institute	d	The Victory Rest Home for Weary Millionaires

5.20 Which pub is next to the Rep Theatre?

a	Cul-de-sac	c	Penday
b	Avenue	d	Duel-Carriageway

5.21 A kebab wi' a'hin on it. In which eatery *won't* you find one?

a	Pegasus 2	c	KeechKhebabs
b	Istanbul	d	Marmaris

5.22 What's the name of the French restaurant in the Nethergate?

a	Wulks 'n' Peenz	c	Pepe's
b	André's	d	The Cundee

5.23 What colour is the Mardi Gras nightclub painted?

a	Blue	c	Silver
b	Red	d	Purple

5.24 When on a pub crawl, if you were to stagger out of The Bush and head towards the High Street, which pub would you next encounter?

a	Tackity Baits	c	Jiggery-Pokeries
	Tickety-Boo's	d	The Nabblers Bucket

5.25 What's the name of the café in City Square?

a	A Broon Ain an'a Mulky Ain Ana	c	Twin-City Café
b	Mister Frothy Stuff	d	Number Two's

5.26 Which of the following is *not* a shop in Reform Street?

a	Photo Factory	c	McDonalds
b	Pancake Place	d	Goodfellow and Steven

5.27 Where can you find Huxter's pub?

a	Reform Street	c	Commercial Street
b	Union Street	d	Hilltown

5.28 How many sculptures are stuck on to the flanks of the Overgate Centre?

a	16	c	28
b	3	d	9

5.29 And who designed them?

a	David Wilson	c	Wilson David
b	Jocky Wilson	d	Wilson Picket

5.30 Which 'Champion' enriched the old arcade below the Caird Hall?

a	Bob Champion	c	Boxing Champion Cassius Clay
b	Champion the Wonder Horse	d	Lord Champion of Batteringham

5.31 Where would you find a pyramid on a lavvie?

a	The Pharaoh Isles	c	West Africa
b	West Kirkton	d	Westport

5.32 What is Rabbie Burns sitting on in Albert Square?

a	A chair	c	A tree trunk
b	A beanbag	d	A bucket

5.33 And what does Rabbie hold in his right hand?

a	A book	c	A pipe
b	A pen	d	A hostage

5.34 What is the name of the wooden sculpture at the junction of Old Hawkhill and Hunter Street?

a	*The Arch*	c	*The Bridge*
b	*The Pillar*	d	*The Neck*

5.35 What musical instrument is it said to represent a part of?

a	A cello	c	A piano
b	A banjo	d	A saxophone

5.36 When was the Murrygate pedestrianised?

a	1962	c	1892
b	1982	d	1992

5.37 How high is St Paul's Cathedral?

a	110 feet	c	210 feet
b	310 feet	d	410 feet

5.38 What would you find at the top of Dundee University's Tower building?

a	A swimming pool	c	A café
b	An argument	d	An angry janny

5.39 Prior to its conversion to a pub, what was The Doghouse?

a	A schoolhouse	c	A cathouse
b	A workhouse	d	A sh**house

5.40 Which of the following is *not* an authentic 'Tay Bridge' bar?

a	The Bar	c	Lounge
b	Walnut Lounge	d	Bridge Bar

5.41   Who wrote the song 'Gaels Blue'?

a	Michael Marra	c	Blind Boy Fuller
b	John Lennon	d	Billy McKenzie

5.42   Which hotel is associated with Nosey Parkers?

a	Royal Hotel	c	Tay Hotel
b	Queen's Hotel	d	Hotel el Piyko

5.43   In which of the following bars would you *not* have to descend steps to enter?

a	Art Bar	c	Nether Inn
b	Jute Bar	d	Laings

5.44   How many baker's shops are on Albert Street?

a	2	c	8
b	7	d	5

5.45   What mythical creature stands on top of the Mercat Cross?

a	A haggis	c	A dragon
b	A unicorn	d	An honest man

5.46 Which 'Sea' would you find in the Nethergate?

a	Deep Sea	c	Blue Sea
b	Black Sea	d	Canna See

5.47 Which auction rooms would you find in Ward Road?

a	Bell & Black Label	c	Curr & Dewar
b	Going & Gone	d	Fred & Barnie's

5.48 Where is the University of Abertay's Student Union?

a	The West Marketgait	c	The West Ferry
b	The Wild West	d	The East Craigie

5.49 In the 19th century, what was Dundee also known as?

a	City of Discovery	c	City of Calamity
b	City of Candle Lights	d	City of Dreadful Knights

5.50 Which Cathedral stands adjacent to DCA?

a	St Andrew's	c	St Michael's
b	St Boswell's	d	St Mary's

6

Thonz no Futba!

The competitive sporting activities of everyday Dundonians over the years have varied enormously. Some sports require a rulebook and a committee to function, as in football, for example, but others require no such constraints and are equally rewarding to participants and spectators. Old tenement classics, such as 'See who can produce the longest spittle oot the windee', or other less dangerous activities like 'Pitch and Toss' or the quick-runners' favourite, 'Last ain to get there's a Jessie', can get the adrenalin flowing much in the same way as it does in professional athletes.

Sport would not be sport if it never involved a bob or twa. The conjoined twin of the sporting fraternity, and by far the wealthier, is, of course, gambling. Yes, the good old bookies. The Coupon. Spot the Ba. Even Pitch and Toss could quickly empty your pockets of small change if you weren't up to scratch on the day of the competition. Conjoined though they may be, they cannot nowadays be separated by the other purse in the world of sports. Not the winning purse but the purse of sponsorship handouts and of appearance money for the more famous athlete. In a bid to find our more about the mysterious world of 'sporting' buckshee handouts, I went and got Liz McColgan's accountant's apprentice mingin' drunk and arranged to have a series of compromising photos taken of him keeping company with a crowd of self-confessed Jessies. Sporting, don't you think? Unfortunately, real info on the world of spare dosh was thin on the track and all he'd say was that it involved more money than a Swiss banker can shake an alpine horn at.

That said, even if you were to become reigning world champion for gochlin oot the windee, I doubt very much if you are ever likely to receive anything other than a bollocking for appearing at the windee, never mind a bob or twa!

6.1 What is the name of Dundee's present ice hockey team?

| a | Dundee Sticks | c | Dundee Stars |
| b | Dundee Puckers | d | Dundee Slaivers |

6.2 Which football team's home ground is Thompson Park?

| a | Dundee FC | c | Dundee United |
| b | Lochee United | d | Lochee Harp |

6.3 Where can you buy 'Arabwear'?

| a | From an Arab | c | From a Dundee United supporter |
| b | From United Stores | d | From United Direct |

6.4 Dick McTaggart won Olympic gold at which games?

| a | Melbourne | c | Melgibson |
| b | Mel B | d | Mel C |

6.5 For which sporting event did he win the gold medal?

| a | Rowing | c | Necking |
| b | Chewing | d | Boxing |

6.6 When was Dens Park officially opened?

a	1899	c	1900
b	1999	d	2000

6.7 Who did Dundee FC play to commemorate their centenary?

a	Dundee United	c	Glasgow Rangers
b	Aris Thesolonika	d	Real Madrid

6.8 Dundee United's first match ended in a 3–0 defeat against which team?

a	Forfar	c	Dumbarton
b	Forres Mechanics	d	Dundee FC

6.9 Which Scottish international goalkeeper was player/manager of DUFC?

a	Hamish McAlpine	c	Paul Sturrock
b	Jim McLean	d	Jimmy Brownlie

6.10 'Our Boys' and 'East-End' amalgamated to form which football team?

a	Dundee	c	Lochee United
b	Dundee United	d	Violet

6.11 When was Dundee FC's first match played?

a	1873	c	1893
b	1899	d	1898

6.12 Who did they play?

a	Forfar Athletic	c	Buckie Thistle
b	Dundee United	d	Glasgow Rangers

6.13 And what was the score?

a	3–3	c	3–2
b	1–2	d	1–3

6.14 Which is the oldest Scottish junior football club?

a	Lochee Boys	c	Edinburgh Elevens
b	East Craigie	d	Dundee Boys

6.15 Dundee United FC were once called, Dundee what?

a	Hearts	c	Hibs
b	Celts	d	Picts

6.16 Who became the longest serving football club manager in Britain?

a	Bob Shankly	c	Kevin Keegan
b	Jim McLean	d	Jimmy Brownlie

6.17 Prior to managing his long-term club, which football team did he play for?

a	Dundee FC	c	Dundee United
b	Glasgow Rangers	d	Forres Mechanics

6.18 What was Dundee United FC's Paul Sturrock fondly known as?

a	Beefy	c	Sleeky
b	Lanky	d	Luggie

6.19 Which prestigious Cup did Dundee United win in 1994?

a	Carling Cup	c	UEFA Cup
b	European Cup	d	Scottish Cup

6.20 And who was DUFC's manager when they won the Cup?

a	Jim McLean	c	Paul Sturrock
b	Ivan Golac	d	Jimmy Golac

6.21 The Dundee Whalers represent which sport?

a	Angling	c	Whaling
b	Seal Hunting	d	American football

6.22 And where is their home ground?

a	Dens Park	c	Riverside Park
b	Caird Park	d	Lochee Park

6.23 Which Dundonian boxed for the English national team before he was honoured by Scotland?

a	Ned Lynch	c	Freddie Tennant
b	Frank Gilfeather	d	Dick McTaggart

6.24 Which royal honour did he receive?

a	CBE	c	MBE
b	CBBC	d	Order of the Golden Mitts

6.25 Which local runner won Commonwealth gold medals in 1986 and 1990?

a	Liz McColgan	c	Gail Pope
b	Lester Gofehstir	d	Kerry Lynch

6.26 What was Premierland?

a	A nightclub	c	A stadium
b	An area for posh folk to get away from the scruffs	d	A soup kitchen

6.27 In the 1930s, who became the youngest and smallest professional boxer in the country?

a	Dick McTaggart	c	Benny Lynch
b	Freddie Tennant	d	John (Nippy Sweetie) Lynch

6.28 And how old was he when he turned pro?

a	18	c	12
b	21	d	15

6.29 How far did he walk to take part in his first 'paid' bout and get home again?

a	140 miles	c	1 mile
b	50 miles	d	100 miles

6.30 And in 1933, he walked to Glasgow to beat whom?

a	His brother	c	Benny Lynch
b	King Kong	d	Big Daddy

6.31 Freddie and Norman Tennant were the only brothers to hold which national boxing championship title?

a	British Bantamweight Championship	c	Scottish Heavyweight Championship
b	Scottish Flyweight Championship	d	British Zipfly Championship

6.32 Name Dundee Football Club's top-scoring legend?

a	Gavin Rae	c	Alan Gilzean
b	Billy Steel	d	Alex Hamilton

6.33 Former DUFC manager Jim McLean coached which team prior to his move to Tannadice?

a	Dundee FC	c	Lochee Boys
b	Forfar Athletic	d	Lochee United

6.34 Who is honoured as DUFC's top scorer?

a	Dave Narey	c	Johnny Coyle
b	Peter McKay	d	Luggie

6.35 Where were the old Imperial Billiard Rooms?

a	Mains Loan	c	Wellgate
b	Hilltown	d	High Street

6.36 Where is the Castle Green Leisure Centre?

a	Glamis	c	Broughty Ferry
b	Lochee	d	Stobswell

6.37 In 1946, brothers John, Ned and Andy Lynch established which multi-sport club?

a	Lochee Boys	c	Olympia
b	Dudhope	d	Longforgan Lassies

6.38 And which city council facility is dedicated to the sporting brothers?

a	The City Chambers	c	The Lynch Sports Centre
b	The Lochee Baths	d	Camperdown Park

6.39 In which league do the Dundee Whalers play?

a	National Budweiser UK	c	International Diamond White
b	Inter-Continental Buckfast	d	Miller Lite UK

6.40 Which brothers joined Dundee FC in 2000?

a	Bohemian	c	Blahardian
b	Bonetti	d	Confetti

6.41 Where are the annual National Hang-Gliding Championships held?

a	Glen Close	c	Glenshee
b	Glen Agnes	d	Glen Campbell

6.42 Which of the following does *not* have a rugby pitch?

a	Dudhope	c	Dawson
b	Downfield	d	Riverside

6.43 Which rugby player became Dundee High's first international prop?

a	Andy Nicol	c	George Ritchie
b	Chris Rea	d	David Leslie

6.44 Which Dundee cycling club took the first three places in the Scottish Veteran Time Trial in 1994?

a	Dundee Wheechers	c	Dundee Wheelers
b	Dundee Whirlies	d	Dundee Walkers

6.45 In the 1983/4 season, what did the Scottish rugby team win for the first time in 50 years?

a	Grand Slam	c	Grand Slag
b	Grand Ma	d	Grand weather wir hayin

6.46 And which Dundonian player subsequently became European Player of the Year?

| a | George Ritchie | c | Chris Rea |
| b | David Leslie | d | Andy Nicol |

6.47 Which Dundonian golfer qualified for the 1959 Open at Muirfield at the age of 15?

| a | Sam Torrance | c | Bob Monkhouse |
| b | Jimmy Tarbuck | d | Bobby Walker |

6.48 And which cup did he win when he was 18?

| a | Scottish Professional Championship | c | British Amateur Championship |
| b | Angus Regional Championship | d | Glenegles Open Championship |

6.49 Who were the golfing brothers that came out of Monifeith to win a string of cups?

| a | Bob and Watty Skite | c | Ian and Fred Hutcheon |
| b | The Broon Twins | d | Vince and Elenor Chalmers |

6.50 Which Dundee sports complex hosted the 1997 Indoor European Club Hockey Championships?

| a | Dundee International Sports Complex | c | Lochee Esoteric Hockey Club |
| b | The Lynch Sports Centre | d | Douglas Sports Centre |

7

Music, Ehrt and Cul'yir

From St Mary's to Magdalen Green, and from Barnhill to Menzieshill, Dundee is teeming with creative talent – from the West Kirkton guitar licks of Kevin Murray to the Fintry spoon soloist himself, Saint Andrew, through the Fleming Gardens soulful vocals of Dougie Martin, all the way to the river and the beauty of brush that is forever James McIntosh Patrick.

If there's one thing you should know about Dundonians, it's their love of expression, whether through music, painting (without the decorating), writing, acting, dancing, singing or just slipping out a wisecrack at somebody else's expense. Dundonians seem to be well endowed in the 'dab hand' department and even the smallest of housing schemes can yield a bumper crop of bohemians year on year.

Luckily, Duncan of Jordanstone College of Art happily sits back and soaks up any directionless local talent and spits out confident creative artists. But, overall, local talent is nurtured mainly by local talent. I'll give you an example . . . A young Glaswegian guy, first year ehrt student at D of J, after checking out which city centre pubs are the best for live music, quickly gets hooked on the big sound of local music legends, Mafia. A few weeks later and the guy plucks up the courage to talk to the soul don, Dougie Martin. He tells Dougie that he has a set of congas that he's been newly getting to grips with. Dougie persuades the guy to play with Mafia the following Saturday. It's in the Caird Hall. It's the guy's first ever gig. And it turns out not to be his last.

Such is the nurturing nature of the city's natural talent.

7.1 Dundee Rep is in which square?

a	Tay Square	c	Leg Square
b	Ankle Square	d	Hip or Square

7.2 Which flower appears on Dundee's coat of arms?

a	The poppy	c	The bluebell
b	The lilly	d	The tulip

7.3 Which fabulous creatures are also on the coat of arms?

a	Sabre-toothed tigers	c	Dragons
b	Dodos	d	Fairies

7.4 In which month is Broughty Ferry Gala Week?

a	January	c	September
b	May	d	July

7.5 What is the name of the stainless-steel kinetic sculpture by Alastair White, which stands at the foot of the Marketgait?

a	*Strange Attractor II*	c	*Fatal Attractor IV*
b	*Usual Repellor III*	d	*Broken Tractor (the original)*

7.6 Which Dundee artist was best known for his landscape paintings of the city and its hinterland, and has had works included in the Royal Scottish Academy?

a	Alberto Morrocco	c	David McLure
b	James Howie	d	McIntosh Patrick

7.7 When was the DCA opened?

a	1999	c	2000
b	2001	d	1998

7.8 Which Dundee-based internationally best-selling novelist is best known for *The Shell Seekers*?

a	W.N. Herbert	c	Rosamunde Pilcher
b	James Meek	d	Leon Uris

7.9 What was the name of Alan Spence's award-winning stage portrayal of the Timex dispute?

a	*On the Line*	c	*On the Broo*
b	*On the Cadge*	d	*On the Up and Up*

7.10 In which play did Joanna Lumley star at the Rep Theatre?

a	*The Cotton Pickers*	c	*The Apple Orchard*
b	*The Cherry Orchard*	d	*The Berry Pickers*

7.11 Which Dundee poet's first collection, *No Hiding Place*, was published in 1996 by Bloodaxe Books?

a	Don Paterson	c	William McGonagall
b	John Burnside	d	Tracey Herd

7.12 When was Dundee's Botanic Gardens established?

a	1971	c	1877
b	1946	d	1957

7.13 Which of the following cities has *not* been twinned with Dundee?

a	Orleans (France)	c	Nablus (Palestine)
b°	Dundee (Jamaica)	d	Zadar (Croatia)

7.14 What is the garden in Albert Square dedicated to?

a	Peace	c	War
b	Famine	d	Slavery

7.15 Which 'Frank' is said to have drunk at the Phoenix Bar after playing at the Caird Hall?

a	Frank Incense	c	Frank Sinatra
b	Frank who works behind the counter in Grouchos	d	Frank (ly m'dear, I don't give a damn)

7.16 What art gallery was opened in the Nethergate in 1999?

a	Princess Gallery	c	Dukes Gallery
b	Lords Gallery	d	Queens Gallery

7.17 Where is the only city centre cinema?

a	The Overgate Centre	c	UGC
b	DCA	d	The Fleapit

7.18 When did the Rep Theatre move to its purpose-built venue?

a	1892	c	1982
b	1922	d	1966

7.19 Where would you find a model of Buzz Aldrin walking on the moon?

a	On the moon	c	In a mill
b	In his bedroom	d	Mills Observatory

7.20 Where is Chris Biddlecombe's sculpture, *Eight-Person Kissing Compass*?

a	Camperdown Park	c	Caird Hall
b	The airport	d	McManus Galleries

7.21 What's the name of Dundee's science centre?

a	Senses	c	Super-Dooper
b	Sensation	d	Sensational

7.22 Which controversial computer simulation series was the brainchild of a Dundee-based company?

a	*Grand Theft Auto*	c	*Bank Job Retro*
b	*Blow Rob Gotcha*	d	*Pub Crawl Junkies*

7.23 Name the largest and best-preserved medieval parish kirk in Scotland?

a	St Patrick's	c	St Pius
b	St Christopher's	d	St Mary's

7.24 When was the neoclassical Camperdown House built?

a	1828	c	1882
b	1922	d	1982

7.25 Which 'Wall' of public art by David Wilson runs South from the Nethergate?

a	Sea Wall	c	Wave Wall
b	Dock Wall	d	Max Wall

7.26 Alistair Smart designed the bronze sculpture of which local mythical creature?

a	A dragon	c	A haggis
b	An honest politician	d	A humorous doctor

7.27 What is Toc-H?

a	A shop	c	A nutcase
b	A radio station	d	A TV sitcom

7.28 'Eh ken sumhin!' was the mantra of the sweeper, Erchy, in which sell-out musical?

a	*The Lady and the Tramp*	c	*The Kilty Cald-Dowps*
b	*The Bum's-Rush*	d	*The Mill Lavvies*

7.29 Who wrote the show?

a	Chris Rattray	c	Gordon Burnside
b	Hamish Glen	d	A cast of thousands

7.30 And who composed the music?

a	Gordon Dougall	c	Michael Marra
b	The Pan-Loafy Quartet	d	Jack Bruce

7.31 Which Dundee music promoter first coined the phrase 'Beatlemania'?

a	Andy Lothian	c	Andy Broon
b	Andy Pelc	d	Andy Pandy

7.32 Which Scottish poet once described Dundee as a 'great industrial cul-de-sac'?

a	William McGonagall	c	Robert Burns
b	Hugh MacDiarmid	d	Don Paterson

7.33 Which Dundee band supported the Beatles at the Caird Hall?

a	The Vikings	c	The Picts
b	The Battered	d	The Poor Souls

7.34 Name the artist who collaborated with Creative Dundonians to produce a muilt-media version of Mussorgsky's *Pictures from an Exhibition*?

a	James McIntosh Patrick	c	Edmund Caswell
b	Vince Rattray	d	John Hood

7.35 Name the Michael Marra song that sees the world through the eyes of singer Dougie Martin's dog?

a	'Julius'	c	'Jeepers'
b	'Jazza'	d	'Jings'

7.36 Who teamed up with St Andrew to write a song for TV personality Selina Scott?

a	Mathew Kelly	c	Stuart (Lonesome Guitar) Ivans
b	Eddie (L'il Chopin) Marra	d	'Wild Man' McGlone

7.37 Who wrote 'Proud to be an Arab'?

a	Ricky Ross	c	Micky Most
b	Randy Newman	d	Randy B*****d

7.38 Who wrote *The Salmon's Tail*?

a	Kevin Murray	c	Kelvin Murphy
b	Kevin Murthly	d	Kreepy Manny

7.39 Who played Dallas in the Woollen Mill's musical version of *Stagecoach*?

a	Jackie Mag	c	Jackie Stuart
b	Jackie McPherson	d	Jackie Wallace

7.40 And what is this person nowadays better known as?

a	Jackie Chan	c	Jackie Bird
b	Jackie Kennedy	d	Wacky-Baccy Jackie

7.41 Which Dundee newspaper featured the hysterical columnist, Showbiz Tam?

a	Standard	c	Lesser
b	Extra	d	The Tele

7.42 What would Ma Broon's first name be?

a	Agnes	c	Martha
b	Margaret	d	Virginia

7.43 Pa Broon once had a nickname. What was it?

a	Shug	c	Pug
b	Lug	d	Smug

7.44 In the stage parody *Dundee Adolescent Showtime*, who played Damien Docherty – King of Knockbacks?

a	Donny Coutts	c	Bonnie Langford
b	Gary Clark	d	John Inman

7.45 Whose life was told in the book *The Glamour Chase*?

a	Dougie Martin	c	Alan Gorrie
b	Jackie Bird	d	Billy McKenzie

7.46 And which Dundonian author wrote it?

a	A. L. Kennedy	c	Tom Doyle
b	John Burnside	d	Rosamund Pilcher

7.47 Which former Danny Wilson member has written songs for Mel C and Natalie Imbruglia, amongst others?

a	Ged Grimes	c	Kit Clark
b	Gary Clark	d	Brian McDermot

7.48 Which artist illustrated *Kidnapped*, *Robinson Crusoe*, *Treasure Island* and *Oliver Twist*?

a	Vince Rattray	c	Belinda Langlands
b	John Cooper-Clark	d	Dudley Dexter Watkins

7.49 Which fictional character is he famed for sketching?

a	Oor Wullie	c	Spiderman
b	The Incredible Hulk	d	Batman

7.50 And where is he supposed to have died?

a	On holiday	c	At his desk
b	In the Bahamas	d	At his auntie's

8

Medicine, Invention, Law and Liberty

The wheel of commerce churns the MILL.

Invention

Some bright-spark invents something the world can't live without. They sell the rights of said invention to a bunch of lawyers and business-suit types. The business-suit types tell their mates and, before you know it, said invention is in every home.

Medicine

After a while, the relationship of folk and said invention begins to wane after reports of no' weel bairns, hair loss and the like filter through the media, and then the possible link between our beloved said invention and such ailments becomes credible.

Law

After many years of legal wrangling, said invention, or rather the next generation of business-suit types, having been found guilty at the High Court of frying the public's brains with said invention and giving them scabs, are ordered to make reparation to the fobbed-off while serving a hefty prison sentence.

Liberty

A few months after, the wind changes direction away from said invention and from the culpable involvement of the business-suited types, the gates of their open prison open and they are spewed out. And them, being resilient business-suited types, are once again soon churning the great commercial MILL for everyone. All they need to do is find the right . . .

Invention

Some bright-spark invents something the world can't live without. They sell the rights of said invention to a bunch of lawyers and business-suit types. The business-suit types tell their mates and, before you know it, said invention is in every home.

The wheel of commerce churns the MILL. That's for sure.

8.1 When was the Wellcome Trust building officially opened in Dundee?

| a | 1997 | c | 1998 |
| b | 1999 | d | 2000 |

8.2 Which 'Sean' donated £40,000 to the Wellcome Trust?

| a | Sean Connery | c | Sean Bean |
| b | Sean the Leprechaun | d | Sean McCannamiyndeeznaim |

8.3 In which field did the Dundee-based scientist Sir James Black become the 1998 Nobel Laureate?

| a | The berry field | c | Medical or physiological |
| b | Genetics | d | The barley field |

8.4 Which fictional character was used in the Ninewells Cancer Campaign?

| a | R2D2 | c | Peter Pan |
| b | Dennis the Menace | d | Sid the Sexist |

8.5 What did Dr Thomas MacLagan discover in 1874?

| a | The planet Jupiter | c | Aspirin |
| b | Gold | d | That his wife had left him because he was never home |

8.6 Where in Dundee did he reside at the time of his discovery?

a	Nethergate	c	Seagate
b	Cowgate	d	Locked oot his ain gate

8.7 And which disease was he hoping to find a cure for at the time of the discovery?

a	Smallpox	c	Regularpox
b	Largepox	d	Rheumatism

8.8 Dr George Alexander Pirie is hailed as one of the early pioneers in what?

a	Amputation	c	X-ray
b	Social clubs for doctors	d	Drag

8.9 Which part of his body is preserved in the city's Ninewells Hospital?

a	His hands	c	His head
b	His feet	d	His other head

8.10 What was the Christian name of the much-praised Dundee surgeon who had Crichton Street named after him?

a	Mathew	c	Mark
b	Luke	d	John

8.11 He was the first doctor in the city to do what?

a	Practise acupuncture	c	Practise sterilisaton
b	Practise on cadavers	d	Practise the quick-step

8.12 Which of the following devices did Dundonian George Louden invent?

a	The umbrella	c	The fixed-focus pocket camera
b	Deep-fat fryer	d	The ironing board

8.13 What book did Mary Godwin begin to write during her years in Dundee, prior to getting married?

a	*Dracula*	c	*Frankenstein*
b	*Wolfman*	d	*The Mummy*

8.14 What year saw the Timex battle?

a	1993	c	1990
b	1996	d	1989

8.15 What did Edward de Garnier bring to Scotland and sell in Dundee's Greenmarket?

a	His daughter	c	His clothes
b	Chips	d	Fish fingers

8.16 What is the surname of the two Dundonian brothers, Preston and James, who are said to have flown a powered aeroplane before the Wright brothers?

a	Watson	c	Wilson
b	Thompson	d	Blitzen

8.17 Which Dundee university was the first to offer degree-level courses in computer-game technology?

a	University of Hard Knocks	c	Dundee University
b	Abertay	d	Sair Tay

8.18 Dundee is reputed to be the world leader in what?

a	Country parks	c	Second-hand dealerships
b	Bank automation	d	Bank overdrafts

8.19 James Thomson proposed which of the following firsts for Britain in 1918?

a	Fresh water supply	c	Outer ring road
b	Income tax	d	First come, first served

8.20 Dundee-based company Trak Microwave built a component for the 1997 NASA Pathfinder mission. Which planet did the mission examine?

a	Neptune	c	Venus
b	Jupiter	d	Mars

8.21 Which of the following has Trak *not* produced components for?

a	Mobile phones	c	Radar
b	Missiles	d	Tonka trucks

8.22 The NCR came to the city in 1947. What does NCR stand for?

a	Non-Commissioned Rejects	c	National Cash Registry
b	National Corporate Retail	d	No Comment Really

8.23 Where did Mrs Keiller's oranges originate?

a	Italy	c	Spain
b	France	d	Tesco

8.24 Which Dundee-based innovator is considered by many to have beaten Edison in making the first constant light using electricity?

a	James Bowman Lindsay	c	Charlie Bowman
b	Cross Bowman	d	Long Bowman

8.25 In which other field was he a great pioneer?

a	Geography	c	Telegraphy
b	Videography	d	Pornography

8.26 What was Dundonian James Chalmers famous for inventing?

a	Lies	c	The rubber dingy
b	The adhesive postage stamp	d	The wheel

8.27 Robert Watson Watt earned a knighthood and the US Medal of Merit for inventing what?

a	A lie-detector test	c	A truth-detector test
b	Junk bonds	d	Radar

8.28 What successful rodent-based 1990s' computer game did Dundee company DMA develop?

a	Rats	c	Guinea Pigs
b	Lemmings	d	Rabbits

8.29 What does DMA stand for?

a	Dundee Moving Animations	c	Developers Make Anything
b	Dinna Mention Autonomy	d	Doesn't Mean Anything

8.30 Which William was the city's superintendent of police in 1844?

a	William Wallace	c	William MacKison
b	William the Lion	d	William of Orange

8.31 And why did he discontinue his post after less than a month?

a	He died	c	He resigned as a protest to corruption
b	He was arrested for being a known conman	d	He was sacked after he was found naked in a local park

8.32 What was the reason for the victorious celebration in 1831 that led to the Town House being overrun, after some of the crowd had been arrested?

a	The vote was extended	c	The city legalised gambling
b	The police went on strike for a day	d	The Provost declared a tax-free week

8.33 And what did John Hume, Dundee's superintendent, do in response to the riotous situation?

a	He sang the 'Halleluiah Chorus'	c	He bolted out the back door and went into hiding
b	He went home greetin for his ma	d	He held his thumbs up to the crowd and shouted, 'Chaps!'

8.34 Which lord once referred to Dundee as a 'sink of atrocity that no amount of moral flushing seems capable of cleansing'?

a	Lord Dundee	c	Lord Cockburn
b	Lord Muck	d	Lord Skinterse

8.35 Why did the city build a new £12,000 prison in the mid-1800s?

a	The old one was burned down	c	The old prison was full to capacity
b	Folk kept escaping from the previous gaol	d	The head turnkey won the lottery

8.36 Dame Margaret Kidd became Scotland's first female what?

a	Police officer	c	Sheriff
b	Bouncer	d	Football referee

8.37 What was the name of the Dundee woman arrested for spying for the Nazis?

a	Jessie James	c	Jessie Jackson
b	Jessie Jordan	d	Jessie Boy

8.38 What did Dundee prohibit in 1778?

a	Alcohol	c	Swearing
b	Vagrancy	d	Slavery

8.39 When was the city's first sheriff appointed?

a	1831	c	1931
b	1731	d	1631

8.40 Who was the last man to be hanged in Dundee Prison?

a	William Bury	c	Bury William
b	Henry Hanger	d	William Dangler

8.41 Who, according to local legend, is he believed to have been?

a	Jock Tamson	c	Jack the Ripper
b	John the Stripper (painter and decorator)	d	Joey the Chipper

8.42 For which act of bravery did PC John R. Little have his 15 minutes of fame?

a	He lifted a double-decker bus off a trapped toddler	c	He swam half a mile into the River Tay to save a whale
b	He took the place of hostages who were being held at gunpoint	d	He was on *Jim' ll Fix It*

8.43 What was George Kinloch outlawed for suggesting?

a	Higher wages for working overtime	c	Common folk should be given the vote
b	A free health service	d	Licence fees for dogs

8.44 Why did Dundee weaver George Mealmaker get sent to Botany Bay?

a	For widdling in the street	c	For sketching anti-English graffiti
b	For writing an anti-war pamphlet	d	For painting an unflattering canvas of the king

8.45 Which of the following did the government refuse to fund, in spite of a recommendation from a Royal Commission?

a	A scheme for public toilets	c	A university for Dundee
b	A public transport system	d	A school for the children of Dundee's wealthy citizens

8.46 Which 'Knight' gained his freedom from slavery in the Dundee courts?

a	The Black Knight	c	Sir Spewalot
b	Joseph Knight	d	Vince Knight

8.47 Who was dragged from his house and forced to dance around the 'Tree of Liberty' shouting 'Liberty and equality forever'?

a	Provost Alexander Riddoch	c	David Couper Thomson
b	Winston Churchill	d	John Cooper Clark

8.48 And what did he do to the symbolic tree the next day?

a	Threw it in the town jail	c	Set it on fire
b	Peed on it	d	Sent it a love letter

8.49 And where was a new ash tree planted in 1986 to commemorate the occasion?

a	Camperdown Park	c	City Square
b	The Botanical Gardens	d	The grounds of the Art College

8.50 What did Dundonian William Anderson invent in 1913?

a	The paperclip	c	The 'silent' ball and stopcock lavatory cistern
b	Dundee cake	d	The automatic toothbrush

Mills, Marmalade and Monday's Paper

For over a century Dundee has lived with the three 'J's of jute, jam and journalism, dominating the less fortunate, or less noticed, commercial enterprises that have kept the city people half-decently solvent. Enterprises like shipbuilding and its ancillary workforce. Enterprises like the Timex factories, which employed thousands of mums and even a few dads. And who can forget the tens of thousands of building tradesmen who have earned their wages by providing most of the city with half-decent homes.

Nowadays, jute mills have been replaced with two-bed flats and the jam baron's factory has now been replaced with a bargain-basement shopping centre. The only original 'J' left holding its own in the 21st century is that of journalism. But even then, it's almost a shadow of its former glorious self. Still huge in the publishing sector of weeklies, dailies and monthlies, DC Thomson persistently reigns supreme. And, if you don't believe me, then just ask Pa Broon.

The rhetoric of jute, jam and journalism seems now to be surpassed by the three 'G's of genetics, gadgets and graduates, and the city is now gripped in the springtime of new technologies. The weaving looms have been replaced by call centres dependant on employees who have bladders with an inordinate capacity. The factory smells of marmalade and sweeties of the past have been sidelined in favour of computer chips, and reading the evening paper has almost been replaced by writing dissertations. Such is the modern city of Dundee we live in today.

9.1 What is supposed to inhabit the Coffin Mill?

a	People	c	A ghost
b	Coffins	d	Rats

9.2 Which of the following *isn't* a jute-making process?

a	Beaming	c	Weaving
b	Spinning	d	Necking

9.3 Which of these has *not* been a jute mill?

a	Bowbridge Works	c	Caldrum Works
b	Verdant Works	d	Weavers Works

9.4 Where was 'The Tipp'?

a	Lochee	c	Broughty Ferry
b	Ninewells	d	Downfield

9.5 By the turn of the 20th century, how much was the average weekly wage for the valuable Dundee weaver?

a	1 pound 4 shillings (£1.20)	c	6 pounds 10 shillings (£6.50)
b	12 shillings (60p)	d	2 shillings and sixpence (12 1/2p)

9.6 Why is the 'Coffin Mill' so called?

a	It used to store coffins	c	It constructed coffins as a side-line
b	The building is shaped like a coffin	d	It was a necromancers' club

9.7 In which street was Dundee's last industrial jute mill situated?

a	Morgan Street	c	Main Street
b	Alexander Street	d	Victoria Road

9.8 From which country did Dundee get its raw jute?

a	Persia	c	China
b	Russia	d	India

9.9 Which of these buildings was Dundee's (and Europe's) largest factory in the 1860s?

a	Keillers	c	Camperdown Works
b	The Coffin Mill	d	Gourley's Shipbuilding Yard

9.10 And how many workers did it employ at that time?

a	14,000	c	30,000
b	2,600	d	7,900

9.11 What percentage of Dundonians were considered unemployed in the 1930s?

a	10%	c	17%
b	22%	d	30%

9.12 From which country did Dundee import flax, prior to the Crimean War?

a	America	c	Russia
b	South Africa	d	Germany

9.13 When was the Coffin Mill constructed?

a	1801	c	1901
b	1928	d	1828

9.14 Which of the following was *not* a Dundee political newspaper?

a	*Dundee Chronical*	c	*Dundee Red Radical*
b	*The Independent*	d	*Dundee Reformer and Lochee Observer*

9.15 What is the name of the 282ft jute works chimney that towers over Lochee?

a	Cox's Stack	c	Cox's Stick
b	Cox's Shaft	d	Cox's Lum

9.16 And when was it built?

| a | 1785 | c | 1965 |
| b | 1865 | d | 1885 |

9.17 King Kaluka was once granted 200 shares in a Dundee investment company, but where was his kingdom?

| a | Fife | c | Hawaii |
| b | Fiji | d | Canada |

9.18 Dundee Land Investment Co. ceded 125 acres of New Mexico land to the US in the 1940s. What did the Yanks use the land for?

| a | To film cowboy movies | c | To plant crops |
| b | To plant orchards | d | Atomic weapons testing |

9.19 Which of the following was *not* processed in Dundee in the late 1700s?

| a | Sugar | c | Glass |
| b | Toilet rolls | d | Snuff |

9.20 What was traditionally used to soften jute fibres in Dundee in the 19th and 20th centuries?

| a | Butter | c | Sheep's urine |
| b | Comfort | d | Whale oil |

9.21 What came to Dundee in 1793?

a	Flax-spinning mills	c	Shipbuilding
b	Tax collectors	d	Law and order

9.22 Which mill was completed by Halley & Brough in 1836?

a	Dens Mill	c	Wallace Craigie Mill
b	Baxter's Mill	d	Coffin Mill

9.23 Which artificial fibre replaced jute in post-WW2 Dundee?

a	Polypropylene	c	Polystyrene
b	Polywannacracker	d	Polly is a cracker

9.24 Between 1841 and 1861, what rose in Dundee by 30,000?

a	The town's debt	c	Cases of in-growing pockets
b	The population	d	The provost's wages

9.25 And how many new houses were built during that 20-year period?

a	16,000	c	30,000
b	942	d	568

9.26 Who was the Dundonian banker whose grandson created James Bond?

a	Peter de Flesher	c	Robert L. Fleming
b	Bob du Flegger	d	Janice P. Squint

9.27 Which of the following countries gave Dundee the fiercest competition in jute production?

a	The USA	c	France
b	China	d	India

9.28 Which of these is a river in Calcutta?

a	Hoogly	c	Shoogly
b	Woogly	d	Tay

9.29 The largest ship ever to sail into the Tay did so in 1863. What was its name?

a	The Edinburgh	c	The Glasgow
b	The Dundee	d	The Perth

9.30 Which roll-on-roll-off ferry service closed in 1985?

a	Dundee–Fife	c	Dundee–Perth
b	Dundee–Oslo	d	Dundee–Rotterdam

9.31 Where in Dundee was the first steam-driven mill built?

a	Benvie Road	c	Guthrie Street
b	Dock Street	d	Hilltown

9.32 Which of the following was *not* greatly invested in by the plutocratic merchants of Dundee in the 19th century?

a	US railways	c	Cattle ranching
b	Hawaii	d	Tackling poverty in Dundee

9.33 What was the 'Piper o' Dundee'?

a	A political newspaper	c	A steam engine
b	A Keiller's fruit preserve	d	A character in *The Dandy*

9.34 When did the *People's Journal* cease circulation?

a	1995	c	1990
b	1988	d	2001

9.35 Which of the following newspapers were *not* owned by John Leng?

a	*People's Journal*	c	*Evening Telegraph*
b	*Dundee Hammer and Sickle*	d	*People's Friend*

9.36 What was the motto of the United Scotsmen movement?

| a | 'Scotland Forever' | c | 'Scotland Free or a Desert' |
| b | 'Scots of the World Unite' | d | 'They May Take Our Lives But They'll Never Take Our Freedom' |

9.37 Why were 18th-century Dundonians required to place a lit candle in their windows once a year?

| a | For Lent | c | To celebrate Christmas |
| b | To celebrate the monarch's birthday | d | To commemorate the death of William Wallace |

9.38 Why did Dundonians celebrate with bell-ringing and bonfires on 13 November 1792?

| a | It was the anniversary of General Monk's death | c | Dundee received city status |
| b | The French revolutionary army made an assault on Brussels | d | Scotland's Parliament merged with England's |

9.39 When did DC Thomson buy the *Evening Telegraph* from the Leng family?

| a | 1906 | c | 1926 |
| b | 1916 | d | 1936 |

9.40 When did *The Dandy* first appear as a comic?

| a | 1945 | c | 1937 |
| b | 1926 | d | 1953 |

9.41 When did *The Beano* first appear as a comic?

a	1938	c	1935
b	1944	d	1964

9.42 With which newspaper did *The Courier* merge?

a	*The Times*	c	*The Piper o' Dundee*
b	*The Advertiser*	d	*The Telegraph*

9.43 Which of the following were returning strike-workers demanded to pledge to DC Thomson's in the late 1920s?

a	To half their wages	c	Never to demand higher wages ever again
b	Never to socialise with workers from another publishing house	d	Never to join a trade union

9.44 What kind of publication was *Bonny Bits*?

a	A political newspaper	c	A cult magazine dedicated to marmalade – with 'bits'
b	A good-news-only newspaper	d	A porno mag

9.45 Who was the Dundonian considered to be the leader of the votes-for-women movement in Scotland?

a	Ethel Moorhead	c	Mary Slessor
b	Mary Keiller	d	Jackie Bird

9.46 What was Dundee's first female trade union?

a	Dundee Women's Union	c	The Dundee and District Mill and Factory Operatives Union
b	The Union of Dundee Women Workers	d	Dundee Women United

9.47 What is the country's oldest magazine?

a	*People's Friend*	c	*The Beano*
b	*The Scots Magazine*	d	*Women's Own*

9.48 When did it begin its print run?

a	1900	c	1800
b	1839	d	1739

9.49 If you were a 'beamer', where would you work?

a	In a weaving mill	c	On a fishing boat
b	In a greenhouse	d	On a building site

9.50 Which of the following was never a DC Thompson's title?

a	*Star Love Stories*	c	*Bimbo*
b	*Bunty*	d	*Dundee Free Press*

10

Missus Lainius Kwehschinz

Many things don't fit neatly into pre-defined categories. Things like the Dundonian guy who was apologising for his dyslexia because he had a misspelt childhood. Things like which is best, plain bread or pan bread? There are a great many things that don't fit neatly into tidy-wrap categories and, for those kind of profound Dundee oddities and others, a home has been found for them here at Chapter 10 (known throughout production of this book as 'the ackwird bugger section').

Here in Chapter 10 we cater for the everyday kind of things that don't conform to the category groove. The kind of things legends are made of. Well, actually, to cut to the chase, this is the chapter where you will find questions on legends. Not just legends but a whole array of juicy stuff as awkward as the day is long. Dragons, Nazis, leaping deer, Chairman Mao, Fred Flintstone, they're all here vying for space in the hinterland of the book's final chapter. Spiced ham might even show up, who knows?

Since this is the final chapter I would like to take this opportunity to wish you the very best of luck with the last 50 questions and, for those who manage to get them all correct, you can share a cheese piece with me any time. Preferably not near the beach, though, on account of me throwing too many dockayz into the water when I was a laddie.

10.1 When the jute industry was at its peak, how many people did it employ in the city?

a	10,000	c	25,000
b	50,000	d	75,000

10.2 How many hours per day were young boys expected to work in the flax mills of the mid-1800's?

a	8–10	c	15–16
b	10–12	d	18–19

10.3 What is the 'Law'?

a	A castle	c	An extinct volcano
b	A book	d	A loch

10.4 How long ago was it formed?

a	1,000 years	c	10 million years
b	50 million years	d	400 million years

10.5 Where is the city's seaside resort?

a	Clatto Park	c	Broughty Ferry
b	Invergowrie	d	Swanny Ponds

10.6 How long is the Dundee Green Circular Cycle Route?

a	26 miles	c	82 miles
b	32 miles	d	2 miles

10.7 What is Dundee's largest park?

a	Dens Park	c	Dudhope Park
b	Camperdown Park	d	Ride 'n' Park

10.8 On which 'Green' can you find a bandstand?

a	Sarah Green	c	Magdalen Green
b	Grass Green	d	Doolee Green

10.9 What year accompanies the Old Clock above the Globe Bar?

a	1998	c	1721
b	1851	d	1864

10.10 Which of the following has never been a Dundee pub?

a	The Bread	c	The Bush
b	The Balcony Bar	d	The Bloody Awful

10.11 What do humpback whales use their 300 baleen plates for?

| a | Feeding | c | Scratching |
| b | Singing | d | Breathing |

10.12 Which museum had a stuffed walrus on display?

| a | McManus | c | The Science Centre |
| b | Barrack Street | d | Broughty Ferry Castle |

10.13 Which Dundee-born actor played Hannibal Lecter in the film *Manhunter*?

| a | Sean Connery | c | Brian Cox |
| b | Anthony Hopkins | d | Robbie Coltrane |

10.14 Which housing scheme has the most saints?

| a | Kirkton | c | Douglas |
| b | St Mary's | d | Linlathen |

10.15 Who was Neddy Scrymgeour?

| a | A politician | c | A pest |
| b | A policeman | d | A pee-the-bed |

10.16 Who did he famously beat at the polls?

a	Ted Heath	c	Winston Churchill
b	Tony Blair	d	Red Rum

10.17 Many Dundee workers were called to and sent from their employment by what?

a	Howkers	c	Chanters
b	Stinkers	d	Bummers

10.18 Which legendary Dundee councillor smuggled funds to the anti-Nazi resistance and the Chinese Red Army?

a	Bob Stewart	c	Bob Roberts
b	Bob the Builder	d	Bob-a-job

10.19 And which notorious leader did he publicly meet in 1955?

a	Ronald Regan	c	Chairman Mao
b	Saddam	d	Che Guevara

10.20 What name was attached to the University of Dundee when it was a university college?

a	Mary Caird	c	Mary Cox
b	Mary Bowbridge	d	Mary Baxter

10.21 What is Scotland's largest art college?

a	Paisley Tech	c	Napier of Edinburgh
b	Duncan of Jordanstone	d	Fred of Flintstone

10.22 What was the name of the Broughty Ferry lifeboat which lost all eight crew in 1959?

a	*The Mona*	c	*The Lisa*
b	*The Mona Lisa*	d	*The Leonardo*

10.23 What was Broughty Ferry once claimed to have been?

a	A posh place	c	The richest square mile in Europe
b	The toe-rag neighbour of Dundee	d	The easiest place to become a millionaire

10.24 What kind of stations were Esplanade and Magdalen Green?

a	Railway stations	c	Cattle stations
b	Police stations	d	Netting stations

10.25 In the recently-built Stack Leisure Park, what do the Venue, Buzz Bar, Busters and Fatty Arbuckle have in common with the multi-screen cinema?

a	They are far too expensive	c	They've closed down
b	They don't have parking spaces	d	They've been demolished

10.26 How many commercial buildings in Stack are still occupied?

| a | 1 | c | 2 |
| b | 3 | d | 4 |

10.27 In which avenue can you see Highland cattle, horses and leaping deer?

| a | Pentland Avenue | c | Balunie Avenue |
| b | Whitfield Avenue | d | Riverside Avenue |

10.28 If you are caught short, and Castle Street lavvies are closed, where would you find the nearest public lav?

| a | Westport | c | West Kirkton |
| b | West Ferry | d | West Hendersons Wynd |

10.29 What has Dundee *never* been?

| a | A dude | c | A dundis |
| b | A deondie | d | A dandie |

10.30 What does 'dun' mean?

| a | Hump | c | Hill |
| b | Hairy | d | Hardy |

10.31 Which earl avoided drowning by being washed-up on the shore at Dundee in 1190?

a	Earl Gray	c	Earl Washington
b	Earl of Strathmore	d	Earl of Huntingdon

10.32 To whom did he dedicate a church?

a	Himself	c	St Mary
b	St Peter	d	St Clement

10.33 Which royal said of Dundee, 'The situation of the town is very fine, but the town itself is not so'?

a	Queen Victoria	c	Queen Elizabeth II
b	Princess Margaret	d	Prince Albert

10.34 In 1881 Lambs Hotel in Reform Street became the first hotel in Britain to do what?

a	Offer a doggie-bag	c	Change the sheets weekly
b	Use electric light	d	Use a flushing toilet system

10.35 Dundee in 1824 saw Scotland's first ever what?

a	UFO	c	Steeplechase horserace
b	Tall ships race	d	Freak show

10.36 Which route did it take?

a	From Riverside to the Law	c	From Glamis to Dundee harbour
b	From the Law to Kinpurnie Castle	d	From one end of the High Street to the other

10.37 Which volcanic feature lies in a field near Myrekirk Road?

a	The Devil's Stone	c	The Devil's Tail
b	The Devil's Plate	d	The Devil's Fiddle

10.38 The remains of which 12th-century Palace of Alexander stands in the Den of Gray?

a	The Burly Broch	c	The Hurly Hawk
b	The Lightning Rod	d	The Eck

10.39 What's the name of the two-ton boulder in the garden of Greystane House?

a	The Pulpit Stone	c	The Pullie Stone
b	The Paddock Stone	d	The Precious Stone

10.40 What relic was unearthed during construction of the Kingsway ring road and is believed to date from the Norse era?

a	Thor's Hammer	c	The Millionaire Stone
b	The Bright Stone	d	The Bullion Stone

10.41 What is carved on the relic?

a	A dragon with a sword in its chest	c	A horseman with a shield and a drinking horn
b	The names of Pictish kings	d	A boy with his finger up his nose

10.42 According to local legend, what is the mysterious Benvie Well said to do?

a	Cure the plague	c	Cure the blind
b	Cure the unfaithful	d	Cure the bacon

10.43 Who was the ghost that told people about the Well?

a	The White Lady of Benvie	c	The Pink Lady of the Seagate
b	The Pious Lady of Church Street	d	The Wayward Lady of Any Street

10.44 What, according to local legend, happened to the Nine Maidens?

a	They all got pregnant	c	They all married the same man
b	They were killed by a dragon	d	They were trampled by a horse

10.45 What does the Latin motto on the city's coat of arms translate as?

a	'God's gift'	c	'The bee's knees'
b	'The wasps nipple'	d	'The dog's bollocks'

10.46 What servants of the crown set upon Dundee whisky smugglers?

a	Grippers	c	Gaugers
b	Grafters	d	Grifters

10.47 According to local folklore, what creature did Jack Jouthers briefly catch in the Tay?

a	A mermaid	c	A whale
b	A cold	d	A sea serpent

10.48 What would you find inside the fruit of a rose bush?

a	Feechee mice	c	Itchy cooz
b	Mingin sheep	d	Randy bulls

10.49 Which area of 'Wells' is close to Menzieshill?

a	Deepwells	c	Blockedwells
b	Ninewells	d	Waterywells

10.50 What is the city's most northern scheme?

a	Whitfield	c	Fintry
b	Kirkton	d	St Mary's

THE ANSWERS

Nooadayz

1.1

c	Fintry

1.2

b	Swanny Ponds

1.3

a	A radio mast

1.4

d	Strathmartine Road

1.5

c	Hilltown

1.6

a	Four

1.7

a	Bucklemaker

1.8

b	Dudhope

1.9

c	Meadowmill

1.10

a	Dundee Business School

1.11

d	Westport

1.12

b	Cowgate

1.13

a	Long Lane

1.14

c	Mills Observatory

1.15

b	Balgay

1.16

a	1935

1.17

c	Biomedical

1.18

d	A pharmacy

1.19

a	Gourdie

1.20

c	Powrie Brae

1.21

c	Michelin

1.22

d	Polepark

1.23

a	Olympia

1.24

b	RSS *Discovery*

1.25

d	Freshly caught fish

1.26

d	Freshly caught fish

1.27

a	2

1.28

c	'Hermless'

1.29

b	A nightclub

1.30

a	Sky High (or 'Skeh Heh')

1.31

d	A group of musicians

1.32

b	Brian Cox

1.33

c	Allan Neave

1.34

a	Kevin Murray

1.35

b	Another Overgate shopping centre

1.36

c	Dougie Martin

1.37

c	Mafia

1.38

a	*Nil Nil*

1.39

d	The Rialto

1.40

c	Hitting a BBC reporter

1.41

a	£16

1.42

b	£17

1.43

d	Visocchi's

1.44

d	In the Nethergate

1.45

a	Town House

1.46

c	Victoria Road

1.47

a	Alan Spence

1.48

b	Ricky Ross

1.49

d	Timex

1.50

a	An album

The Language

2.1

| b | Smelly |

2.2

| b | A chancer |

2.3

| a | A rock |

2.4

| d | A refuse collector |

2.5

| c | A smack |

2.6

| b | Belching |

2.7

| a | A shakaydoon |

2.8

| d | Fainting |

2.9

| d | A dub |

2.10

| a | Bad tempered |

2.11

| d | A pigeon |

2.12

| c | A cundee |

2.13

| b | Tipping it |

2.14

| b | Your bum |

2.15

| d | Barkit |

2.16

| c | A hayvir |

2.17

| b | Sick |

2.18

| c | Horrible and sickly |

2.19

| d | A poolee |

2.20

| d | A hospital |

2.21

| c | Stupid |

2.22

| c | Pot-ugly |

2.23

| b | A toilet |

2.24

| d | A nabbler |

2.25

| c | A pehnday |

2.26

| a | Rotten |

2.27

| d | Contagious |

2.28

| d | A nyaff |

2.29

| d | The fragrance of a sewage worker |

2.30

| c | Vibrating |

2.31

| b | An early morning call |

2.32

| c | A fairdeegowk |

2.33

| d | A fright |

2.34

| b | A vacant facial expression |

2.35

| a | A tenement walkway |

2.36

| d | Spilling something |

2.37

| d | I haven't a clue. |

2.38

| c | A loaf of bread |

2.39

| b | Talking posh |

2.40

| d | Counting |

2.41

| c | Hens |

2.42

| b | A pest |

2.43

| d | Skint |

2.44

| c | Snehct |

2.45

| d | A sparrow |

2.46

| d | Camperdown Park |

2.47

| a | A sweet |

2.48

| c | A kerb |

2.49

| b | A rock |

2.50

| d | Big bubbulee bairn |

The Aldin Days

3.1
| a | Dundee 3 Rangers 1 |

3.2
| b | 1921 |

3.3
| c | Mary Queen of Scots |

3.4
| c | Incorporated Tools |

3.5
| c | Butchers |

3.6
| b | Meeting place |

3.7
| b | Pawnbrokers |

3.8
| a | The Regal |

3.9
| c | A witch |

3.10
| c | At the top of the Wellgate steps |

3.11
| c | Dudhope Park |

3.12
| a | Sir William Wallace |

3.13
| b | Winston Churchill |

3.14
| d | 1956 |

3.15
| c | A Masonic hall |

3.16
| c | Blue Mountains |

3.17
| c | Joiners |

3.18
| a | Cowgate |

3.19
| c | A church and a pub |

3.20
| a | 12th |

3.21
| d | William Wallace |

3.22
| a | Robert the Bruce |

3.23
| a | General Monk |

3.24
| a | Dun Deagh |

3.25
| c | A railway line |

3.26
| a | John Graham of Claverhouse |

3.27
| b | Bonny Dundee |

3.28
| c | Bluidy Claivers |

3.29
| b | Lord Gray |

3.30
| a | The Greens Playhouse |

3.31

d	Beside King William Dock

3.32

b	George Kinloch

3.33

c	Paddy

3.34

d	St Mary's in the Field

3.35

c	A head

3.36

c	The town governor

3.37

b	The Pillars

3.38

d	Hilltown

3.39

b	Backlands

3.40

c	1–2 roomed houses

3.41

a	Infant mortality rate

3.42

c	A tempest

3.43

b	Alpin

3.44

c	The Picts beheaded the king on the King's Cross

3.45

d	A large stone with a circular hole

3.46

b	Jimmy Shand

3.47

a	James Bowman Lindsay

3.48

c	The Palace Theatre

3.49

d	Bonnybank Road

3.50

a	The Progress Hall

The River

4.1
a *Mars*

4.2
c Destitute boys

4.3
c In the McManus Galleries

4.4
a Male

4.5
d Football

4.6
b Seals

4.7
c A ferryboat

4.8
a 1966

4.9
c 1878

4.10
a 1879

4.11
b Antarctic

4.12
d 1901

4.13
d Captain Scott

4.14
a *Unicorn*

4.15
d A war ship

4.16
b Esplanade

4.17
c Dock Stewart's

4.18
a DP& L

4.19
d *Forfar*

4.20
a Grace Darling

4.21
a The Robb Caledon

4.22
c *The Terra Nova*

4.23
d *The Unicorn*

4.24
a Craig Pier

4.25
b *Morning*

4.26
c *The Terra Nova*

4.27
b Ta

4.28
c To melt or flow

4.29
b They were looted by the locals

4.30
d Loch Tay

4.31

| a | 25,734 |

4.32

| a | Two |

4.33

| c | 70 |

4.34

| d | April |

4.35

| a | 117 miles |

4.36

| d | King William's Wharf |

4.37

| c | Wine |

4.38

| b | 3% |

4.39

| d | 1887 |

4.40

| a | 'Address to the new Tay Bridge' |

4.41

| d | Arm & Legg |

4.42

| c | £51,000 |

4.43

| b | Admiral de Winter |

4.44

| a | 1854 |

4.45

| c | £226 |

4.46

| a | He charged Dundonians to view it |

4.47

| c | 1873 |

4.48

| b | Marine Training Centre |

4.49

| d | James McIntosh |

4.50

| c | 7 |

Doon Toon

5.1

| c | 156 feet |

5.2

| c | 2000 |

5.3

| d | Albert Square |

5.4

| b | Verdant Works |

5.5

| b | St Andrews Lane |

5.6

| d | A bell |

5.7

| a | 4 |

5.8

| c | Minnie the Minx |

5.9

| d | 2 |

5.10

| c | Wind |

5.11

| d | Prince Albert |

5.12

| a | The Post Office |

5.13

| c | Admiral Duncan |

5.14

| c | Castle Street |

5.15

| a | 3 |

5.16

| d | The Pillars |

5.17

| c | Ten to eight |

5.18

| a | St Mary's Gate |

5.19

| b | The Albert Institute |

5.20

| a | Cul-de-sac |

5.21

| c | KeechKhebabs |

5.22

| b | André's |

5.23

| d | Purple |

5.24

| b | Tickety-Boo's |

5.25

| c | Twin-City Café |

5.26

| d | Goodfellow and Steven |

5.27

| a | Reform Street |

5.28

| c | 28 |

5.29

| a | David Wilson |

5.30

| b | Champion the Wonder Horse |

5.31

d	Westport

5.32

c	A tree trunk

5.33

b	A pen

5.34

c	*The Bridge*

5.35

a	A cello

5.36

d	1992

5.37

c	210 feet

5.38

c	A café

5.39

a	A schoolhouse

5.40

d	Bridge Bar

5.41

a	Michael Marra

5.42

b	Queen's Hotel

5.43

c	Nether Inn

5.44

d	5

5.45

b	A unicorn

5.46

a	Deep Sea

5.47

c	Curr & Dewar

5.48

a	The West Marketgait

5.49

d	City of Dreadful Knights

5.50

a	St Andrew's

Thonz no futba!

6.1
| c | Dundee Stars |

6.2
| b | Lochee United |

6.3
| d | From United Direct |

6.4
| a | Melbourne |

6.5
| d | Boxing |

6.6
| a | 1899 |

6.7
| b | Aris Thesolonika |

6.8
| c | Dumbarton |

6.9
| d | Jimmy Brownlie |

6.10
| a | Dundee |

6.11
| c | 1893 |

6.12
| d | Glasgow Rangers |

6.13
| a | 3–3 |

6.14
| b | East Craigie |

6.15
| c | Hibs |

6.16
| b | Jim McLean |

6.17
| a | Dundee FC |

6.18
| d | Luggie |

6.19
| d | Scottish Cup |

6.20
| b | Ivan Golac |

6.21
| d | American football |

6.22
| b | Caird Park |

6.23
| d | Dick McTaggart |

6.24
| c | MBE |

6.25
| a | Liz McColgan |

6.26
| c | A stadium |

6.27
| b | Freddie Tennant |

6.28
| d | 15 |

6.29
| a | 140 miles |

6.30
| c | Benny Lynch |

6.31

b	Scottish Flyweight Championship

6.32

c	Alan Gilzean

6.33

a	Dundee FC

6.34

b	Peter McKay

6.35

d	High Street

6.36

c	Broughty Ferry

6.37

a	Lochee Boys

6.38

c	The Lynch Centre

6.39

a	National Budweiser UK

6.40

b	Bonetti

6.41

c	Glenshee

6.42

a	Dudhope

6.43

c	George Ritchie

6.44

c	Dundee Wheelers

6.45

a	Grand Slam

6.46

b	David Leslie

6.47

d	Bobby Walker

6.48

a	Scottish Professional Championship

6.49

c	Ian and Fred Hutcheon

6.50

a	Dundee International Sports Complex

Music, Ehrt and Cul'yir

7.1

| a | Tay Square |

7.2

| b | The lilly |

7.3

| c | Dragons |

7.4

| d | July |

7.5

| a | *Strange Attractor II* |

7.6

| d | McIntosh Patrick |

7.7

| a | 1999 |

7.8

| c | Rosamunde Pilcher |

7.9

| a | *On the Line* |

7.10

| b | *The Cherry Orchard* |

7.11

| d | Tracey Herd |

7.12

| a | 1971 |

7.13

| b | Dundee (Jamaica) |

7.14

| a | Peace |

7.15

| c | Frank Sinatra |

7.16

| d | Queens Gallery |

7.17

| b | DCA |

7.18

| c | 1982 |

7.19

| d | Mills Observatory |

7.20

| a | Camperdown Park |

7.21

| b | Sensation |

7.22

| a | *Grand Theft Auto* |

7.23

| d | St Mary's |

7.24

| a | 1828 |

7.25

| c | Wave Wall |

7.26

| a | A dragon |

7.27

| b | A radio station |

7.28

| d | *The Mill Lavvies* |

7.29

| a | Chris Rattray |

7.30

| c | Michael Marra |

7.31

a	Andy Lothian

7.32

b	Hugh MacDiarmid

7.33

d	The Poor Souls

7.34

c	Edmund Caswell

7.35

a	'Julius'

7.36

c	Stuart (Lonesome Guitar) Ivans

7.37

a	Ricky Ross

7.38

a	Kevin Murray

7.39

b	Jackie McPherson

7.40

c	Jackie Bird

7.41

a	*Standard*

7.42

b	Margaret

7.43

c	Pug

7.44

a	Donny Coutts

7.45

d	Billy McKenzie

7.46

c	Tom Doyle

7.47

b	Gary Clark

7.48

d	Dudley Dexter Watkins

7.49

a	Oor Wullie

7.50

c	At his desk

Medicine, Invention, Law and Liberty (MILL)

8.1
| c | 1998 |

8.2
| a | Sean Connery |

8.3
| c | Medical or physiological |

8.4
| b | Dennis the Menace |

8.5
| c | Aspirin |

8.6
| a | Nethergate |

8.7
| d | Rheumatism |

8.8
| c | X-ray |

8.9
| a | His hands |

8.10
| d | John |

8.11
| a | Practise acupuncture |

8.12
| c | The fixed-focus pocket camera |

8.13
| c | *Frankenstein* |

8.14
| a | 1993 |

8.15
| b | Chips |

8.16
| a | Watson |

8.17
| b | Abertay |

8.18
| b | Bank automation |

8.19
| c | Outer ring road |

8.20
| d | Mars |

8.21
| d | Tonka trucks |

8.22
| c | National Cash Registry |

8.23
| c | Spain |

8.24
| a | James Bowman Lindsay |

8.25
| c | Telegraphy |

8.26
| b | The adhesive postage stamp |

8.27
| d | Radar |

8.28
| b | Lemmings |

8.29
| d | Doesn't Mean Anything |

8.30
| c | William MacKison |

8.31

| b | He was arrested for being a known conman |

8.32

| a | The vote was extended |

8.33

| c | He bolted out the back door and went into hiding |

8.34

| c | Lord Cockburn |

8.35

| b | Folk kept escaping from the previous gaol |

8.36

| c | Sheriff |

8.37

| b | Jessie Jordan |

8.38

| d | Slavery |

8.39

| a | 1831 |

8.40

| a | William Bury |

8.41

| c | Jack the Ripper |

8.42

| b | He took the place of hostages who were being held at gunpoint |

8.43

| c | Common folk should be given the vote |

8.44

| b | For writing an anti-war pamphlet |

8.45

| c | A university for Dundee |

8.46

| b | Joseph Knight |

8.47

| a | Provost Alexander Riddoch |

8.48

| a | Threw it in the town jail |

8.49

| d | The grounds of the Art College |

8.50

| c | The 'silent' ball and stopcock lavatory cistern |

Mills, Marmalade and Monday's Paper

9.1
| c | A ghost |

9.2
| d | Necking |

9.3
| d | Weavers Works |

9.4
| a | Lochee |

9.5
| b | 12 shillings (60p) |

9.6
| b | The building is shaped like a coffin |

9.7
| a | Morgan Street |

9.8
| d | India |

9.9
| c | Camperdown Works |

9.10
| a | 14,000 |

9.11
| b | 22% |

9.12
| c | Russia |

9.13
| d | 1828 |

9.14
| c | *Dundee Red Radical* |

9.15
| a | Cox's Stack |

9.16
| b | 1865 |

9.17
| c | Hawaii |

9.18
| d | Atomic weapons testing |

9.19
| b | Toilet rolls |

9.20
| d | Whale oil |

9.21
| a | Flax-spinning mills |

9.22
| c | Wallace Craigie Mill |

9.23
| a | Polypropylene |

9.24
| b | The population |

9.25
| d | 568 |

9.26
| c | Robert L. Fleming |

9.27
| d | India |

9.28
| a | Hoogly |

9.29
| b | *The Dundee* |

9.30
| d | Dundee–Rotterdam |

9.31

| c | Guthrie Street |

9.32

| d | Tackling poverty in Dundee |

9.33

| a | A political newspaper |

9.34

| c | 1990 |

9.35

| b | *Dundee Hammer and Sickle* |

9.36

| c | 'Scotland Free or a Desert' |

9.37

| b | To celebrate the monarch's birthday |

9.38

| b | The French revolutionary army made an assault on Brussels |

9.39

| a | 1906 |

9.40

| c | 1937 |

9.41

| a | 1938 |

9.42

| b | *The Advertiser* |

9.43

| d | Never to join a trade union |

9.44

| a | A political newspaper |

9.45

| a | Ethel Moorhead |

9.46

| c | The Dundee and District Mill and Factory Operatives Union |

9.47

| b | *The Scots Magazine* |

9.48

| d | 1739 |

9.49

| a | In a weaving mill |

9.50

| d | *Dundee Free Press* |

Missus Lainius Kwehschinz

10.1
| b | 50,000 |

10.2
| d | 18–19 |

10.3
| c | An extinct volcano |

10.4
| d | 400 million years |

10.5
| c | Broughty Ferry |

10.6
| a | 26 miles |

10.7
| b | Camperdown Park |

10.8
| c | Magdalen Green |

10.9
| d | 1864 |

10.10
| d | The Bloody Awful |

10.11
| a | Feeding |

10.12
| b | Barrack Street |

10.13
| c | Brian Cox |

10.14
| b | St Mary's |

10.15
| a | A politician |

10.16
| c | Winston Churchill |

10.17
| d | Bummers |

10.18
| a | Bob Stewart |

10.19
| c | Chairman Mao |

10.20
| d | Mary Baxter |

10.21
| b | Duncan of Jordanstone |

10.22
| a | *The Mona* |

10.23
| c | The richest square mile in Europe |

10.24
| a | Railway stations |

10.25
| c | They've closed down |

10.26
| b | 3 |

10.27
| d | Riverside Avenue |

10.28
| a | Westport |

10.29
| d | A dandie |

10.30
| c | Hill |

10.31

| d | Earl of Huntingdon |

10.32

| c | St Mary |

10.33

| a | Queen Victoria |

10.34

| b | Use electric light |

10.35

| c | Steeplechase horserace |

10.36

| b | From the Law to Kinpurnie Castle |

10.37

| a | The Devil's Stone |

10.38

| c | The Hurly Hawk |

10.39

| b | The Paddock Stone |

10.40

| d | The Bullion Stone |

10.41

| c | A horseman with a shield and a drinking horn |

10.42

| a | Cure the plague |

10.43

| a | The White Lady of Benvie |

10.44

| b | They were killed by a dragon |

10.45

| a | 'God's gift' |

10.46

| c | Gaugers |

10.47

| a | A mermaid |

10.48

| c | Itchy cooz |

10.49

| b | Ninewells |

10.50

| d | St Mary's |

How Did You Do?

Score	Verdict
500–451	Careful, your pants may be on fire.
451–500	So, brainbox, what else do you do with your time?
351–450	You can certainly class yourself as a real-deal Dundonian, so get somebody to pat you on the back!
251–350	Well done! You know more about this city than most of its inhabitants. By the way, how long have you worked in a library?
151–250	Still a fairly good score but I doubt if you can ask a baker for a 'peh' without being tumbled as an impostor.
51–150	If you live in Dundee, then you should get out of the schemes more. Shame on you, mince for brains!
0–50	Tell the truth, you're not from around these parts, are you?